The American Woman Playwright

For Jennifer Erin

The American Woman Playwright

A View of Criticism and Characterization

by

Judith Olauson

The Whitston Publishing Company
Troy, New York
1981

Library of Congress Catalog Card Number 80-51605
ISBN 0-87875-198-X

Printed in the United States of America

Acknowledgements

Acknowledgement is made to the following for material reprinted by permission:

Lois W. Banner, *Women in Modern America, A Brief History*, Harcourt, Brace, Jovanovich, Inc., 1974.

Clare Boothe, "The Women," in *Plays By and About Women*. New York: Random House, Inc., 1973.

Rosalyn Drexler, "Home Movies," in *The Line of Least Existence and Other Plays*. New York: Random House, Inc., 1967.

Wolcott Gibbs, "A Pamphlet Comes to Town," in *The New Yorker*. 20, No. 13 (13 May 1944), p. 44.

Vivian Gornick, "Who is the Fairest of Them All?" in *The Village Voice*, 15, No. 22 (28 May 1970), p. 47.

Lorraine Hansberry, *A Raisin in the Sun*. 1966, William Morris Agency, Inc. as agents for Lorraine Hansberry and Robert Nemiroff as executor of the estate of Lorraine Hansberry, by Mel Berger.

Lorraine Hansberry, *The Sign in Sidney Brustein's Window*. New York: Random House, Inc., 1965.

Richard Hayes, "The Stage," in *Commonweal*, 59, No. 18 (5 February 1954), p. 449; No. 3 (17 April 1959), p. 301.

Lillian Hellman, *An Unfinished Woman*. Boston: Little, Brown and Company, 1969.

Lillian Hellman, *The Little Foxes*. New York: The Viking Press, 1973.

Lillian Hellman, *Pentimento*. Boston: Little, Brown and Company, 1973.

Lillian Hellman, "Toys in the Attic," in *Six American Plays for Today*, ed. by Bennett Cerf, New York: The Modern Library, Random House, Inc., 1961.

Lillian Hellman, *Watch on the Rhine*. New York: Random House, Inc., 1941.

Myrna Lamb, *The Mod Donna and Scyklon Z*. (By permission of author) [Pathfinder Press, Inc., 1971].

"Five Important Playwrights Talk About Theatre Without Compromise and Sexism," *Mademoiselle*, 75 (August 1972), p. 289. Copyright 1972 by The Condé Nast Publications, Inc.

Burns Mantle, *The Best Plays of 1931-32*, p. 267; *The Best Plays of 1936-37*, p. 218; *The Best Plays of 1940-41*, p. 360; *The Best Plays of 1941-42*, p. 7 and pp. 349-350; *The Best Plays of 1943-44*, p. 315; and *The Best Plays of 1946-47*, p. 163. New York: Dodd, Mead & Company.

Mary McCarthy, *Mary McCarthy's Theatre Chronicles 1937-1962*. (By permission of author) [Farrar, Straus & Giroux, Inc., 1963].

Rochelle Owens, *Futz and What Came After*. (By permission of author) New York: Random House, Inc., 1968.

Preface

Throughout the history of the American theatre, little attention has been paid to women playwrights. A review of theatre criticism found in this study reveals a lack of woman-centered material and theory in character and thematic analysis of serious dramas by women. This apparant neglect of what evolves as a "special" group of writers is intriguing and forms a secondary focus for this study.

But what women themselves present in terms of female universal types is the basic concern of this book. It seems reasonable to explore the problem of the apparent lack of both woman-centered material and theory by examining representative plays written exclusively by women to see if women themselves are offering the material and theory. Over a forty year period, a trend can be seen in the vision of the woman playwright which indicates a change of characterization from the simple, passive, socially subjugated women characters of earlier plays to complicated, active women who attempt, although not always successfully, to become autonomous beings. Also, the playwrights selected herein indicate a wide range of roles for women: social dependents, keepers of society's standards and protectors of its morality, social rebels, confused and deranged paranoiacs, and victims of a male-dominated culture. Their themes encompass identification with domestic difficulties, social ills, personal frustrations and psychic confusion.

Thus it seems that women have gradually achieved a freer expression of a variety of themes and characters throughout four recent decades of their history, a significant evolution within the broader framework of American theatre history since this pattern of change seems to coincide with the changing roles of women in American society.

By focusing this topic of women's view of women, recognizing the facts that have been previously ignored or taken for granted, it is hoped that the old theories of "woman's place" as dramatist in the American theatre can be reappraised and broadened. It is also hoped that this study will represent an attempt to integrate an interest in women as viable, stageworthy individuals who challenge the dominant bias that women's minds and behavior lack order or interest. As a result, the women and their characters studied should illustrate ways in which women think about women in their own search for understanding the world.

The plays selected for this study have been included on the basis of apparent success with audiences or critics; that is, all the plays have sustained a continuous run of at least thirty performances on or off-Broadway stages.

Contents

Chapter I

Background

The emancipation of women in the United States over the past forty years has brought about great changes in the social status of the American woman. From the traditional goals of home, husband, and the attainment of physical beauty, women have advanced to new freedoms ranging from competing with men on an equal basis in business, industry, education, and government, to unrestricted pursuit of sexual fulfillment.

In the past it seemed necessary for a woman to define herself by the relationships she was able to establish with men. Today a woman may choose to define herself as an autonomous, independent, self-sufficient individual, with or without male definition if that is her desire.

The changes brought about by emancipation have been rapid; however, the effects have been slow in being absorbed by the American culture whose traditions originated in patriarchal societies of the past. The rapid revolution, as Seymour Farber and Roger Wilson point out in their study, *The Potential of Woman*, predictably has produced "dislocation and even chaos" in some areas of American society and perhaps with good reason: "We still do not know the practical limits of equality."[1]

For women in the arts this unsettled state of equality has brought a period of transition. The traditional views of the feminine character are being challenged by those who question the relevance to social change of old critical standards; their strongest objection to traditional criticism is that the standards of the past have not yet been adjusted to changes of the present.

The problem of the creative woman seems to be no longer an issue of political equality or equal franchise. Marya Mannes points out in her report on the status of American women in the arts at the University of California symposium, "Man and Civilization," January, 1965, that the end of legal and civil discriminations against women has been "inevitable" and the problems that have arisen from these inequities are in the process of being rectified through legislation.[2] The issue seems to be a deeper, more complex question, that of the acceptance of woman's expression in the arts which may differ from the historically predominant male expression. Obviously this is an issue which cannot be legislated.

In Mannes' view it is no longer a question of whether a woman *should* deviate from the old patterns of life and traditional life styles; the fact is that some women *do*, and they should be recognized for the inherent values they possess as artists no matter how much or how little they vary from traditional male values. Thus a more realistic evaluation of the dilemma of the woman artist appears to be the recognition of critical apathy with which she has been met.

In the literary fields, critical attitudes towards women who are writers form "an untidy subject," in the understated opinion of Michele Murray, author of the critical examination of women in literature, *A House of Good Proportion*.[3] For, in the endeavor of writing, the progress of women has been uneven. Coupled with the "dislocation" and "chaos" of social transmutation, diverse theorizing about what and how women should write and on what basis they should be judged has compounded the problem.

The woman writer has had a long history of struggle for recognition in virtually all areas of literature which she has attempted. Not much has been preserved of what women have written or said throughout history. This critical disregard, declares Virginia Woolf in her essay, *A Room of One's Own*, was precisely the problem for past women writers. In Woolf's view, masterpieces of literature do not just happen but are the product of many years of common thinking. Since women had no past as writers, no recorded precedent to follow, and little encouragement that anything written by a woman before had much literary value, it was difficult for them to find the initiating force enabling them to write honestly of their own thoughts and desires.[4] Moreover, throughout their history, states Woolf, women have never had the economic freedom nor the privacy, as men have had, to create great works.

The ideal conditions which Virginia Woolf viewed as necessary for the development of great women writers are perhaps more readily attainable today. But the attitude apparently remains that, in spite of contemporary redefinition of women's roles in society, woman's place must necessarily be confined to the home, still the theme of many critics. This attitude is certainly an oversimplification today. Michele Murray declares that almost all of the current non-fiction writing on this subject of women is ruled by poverty of imagination, the criticism being based on an expedient "either/or" breakdown: "either a woman made in man's image or a pseudo-man."[5] In view of the gains women have made, this standard of judgment, when applied to women writers today, seems likely to be inappropriate, quaintly prejudicial, and ultimately ill-conceived. Ellen Moers, in her article, "The Angry Young Women," reviews the long-held theories about why women have not, or cannot, achieve as writers. Moers believes that both men and women have been socially conditioned to accept these misconceptions:

1. Women are uncomfortable with facts or big ideas. Their intellectual preoccupations are small.

2. Women's experience is limited to home and hearth.

3. Women are naturally sensitive to smaller emotional states but usually have less perceptive powers than men.

4. Women's natures are passive, not active, and ordinarily they observe rather than do. Therefore, they are more adept at noting detailed social nuances than men; thus they are more conservative, nostalgic, and, at times, brilliantly satiric of small social scenes.

5. Women are able to write short pieces of literature best because they are often interrupted by domestic demands.

6. Women are deficient in logic and order therefore lack the ability to create good plots.[6]

Because generalized attitudes such as these prevail among some critics, women writers often have been patronized, dismissed summarily, or have been absorbed into the mainstream of male art when they seem to conform to the established expectations of what art should be. But the facile distinctions of critics who have found women's writing to be categorically inferior (or, by chance, suprisingly good) seem no longer acceptable. Mary Ellmann, analyzing the present state of female writers in her book *Thinking About Women*, agrees that it is no longer intellectually possible to accomodate these opinions.[7]

Many current works which focus on the problem of this apparent critical injustice suggest that since most successful writing has been created by men and is distinctly from a male standpoint, most criticism is directed toward that dominating view. Louise Bernikow, editor of *The World Split Open*, a volume of poetry by women, discusses the difficulty women have had in finding a place in literary history. She observes that the basic problem for women writers is that they have been conditioned to, and have accepted, stereotyped roles of themselves which are based on patriarchal dicta. This has caused serious problems with their subject matter when they attempt to write. Their place has been strictly defined by the topics which men have designated as being in keeping with their social and psychological roles.[8] She concludes that there has been an overshadowing by the preponderant male perspective of theme, subject matter, and character throughout literary history. Writers and critics, whether male or female, have provided little theory or understanding of the female human condition. Therefore, because of woman's peripheral standing, it is not surprising that she does not contribute fully to the literary and dramatic arts because culture and tradition do not necessarily express her values.

The most likley explanation to the question, why have there been so few great women writers, then, is that some women, according to Rosalind Miles, are still far from attaining the socio-cultural, educational, and economic freedom enjoyed by some men as evidenced by the fact that in many instances, and despite legislation, women are still pressured to conform to traditional patterns of behavior and "are still expected to remain self-effacing, supportive and unjudging."[9]

In assessing the position of women playwrights over the past forty years, the situation seems no more encouraging. In fact, women dramatists are "even more thin on the ground" than women novelists and poets.[10] Miles repeats the popular claim that because playwriting is a more demanding occupation than novel writing, it is a genre which women have avoided. The rationale behind such a claim, she states, is that writing a novel is far less assertive than making a play; therefore, women have had more success as novelists than as playwrights because ostensibly they are deficient in the necessary, aggressive "male" attributes. This reasoning suggests, then, that novel writing is more compatible with the conventional requirement that women should "always keep their heads down," and that playwriting, because it demands total and continuous objectivity, that quality which is "difficult for the feminine mind to achieve or maintain," is not.[11] Indeed, the attraction of women to the novel form is found in the viewpoint of one successful American woman playwright, Lillian Hellman. Hellman expresses an ambivalent view of the playwriting profession in her autobiographical work, *An Unfinished Woman*. Here she intimates that since her initial desire was to be a novelist, she has never been sure why she became a dramatist:

> I started out wanting to write novels and didn't have much interest in the theatre or movies; maybe my own nature does not fit the rushing strong tones of the theatre, although certainly my own tones are often shrill; maybe because I am not good at collaboration, the essence of the theatre; maybe because I like fame, but don't like, and am no good at, its requirements; or maybe vanity of any kind other than my own seems to be at first funny and at last boring. But most of all, the theatre is not a natural world for those who question whatever is meant by glamour. One must, one should, pay fame the respect it demands, or leave it alone and find someplace else to go. I have not been able to do either and thus have often made myself and other people uncomfortable.[12]

Hellman also stated earlier in her career that she felt the theatre was "a tight, unbending, unfluid, meagre form in which to write."[13] Compared to the novel, she stated, the play was a "second-rate form."[14] Considering Hellman's unprecedented success as a playwright in spite of her own apprehensions, Miles' opinion seems tenable, that there is fallacy in reasoning that women lack the strength to meet "the rushing strong tones" which the theatre evidently demands. Miles proposes that social-conditioning is the only factor which makes it seem true. Thus it seems that few women ever attempt playwriting because they have been conditioned to believe that only men can succeed at it; in this "emancipated" twentieth century only Lillian Hellman seems to stand in equal regard with prominent male playwrights, even if more as "a contemporary phenomenon" than as enduring artist.[15] Perhaps because it appears there are so few women playwrights, their work has been judged too small to warrant even the most superficial attention. It is Miles' belief that because criticism, until very recently, has been an entirely male province, it has dealt with creative women by treating them as males; so this special little band of playwrights has been "surrounded and absorbed without trace into the masculine act of making plays."[16]

Miles' explanations of why there have been few great women playwrights have validity and are relevant. But she seems as deficient in her observations as other critics have been in their failure to recognize the fact that there have been and are considerably more women writing for the American theatre than a few obvious figures. Other women have made extensive contributions to the body of American dramatic literature but apparently have been presumed to be second-rate and undeserving of thorough critical attention. For example, in the twentieth century alone, what analysis has been made of the prolific works of Zoe Akins, whose plays spanned a period of time from the early 1900s to the mid-1930s, or of Rachel Crothers who wrote an even greater number of plays over an even longer period of time; and of Rose Franken and Susan Glaspell? In the 1940s and 1950s, Sophie Treadwell, Carson McCullers, Jean Kerr, Mary Chase, Ruth Gordon, Lorraine Hansberry, and Jane Bowles all made significant contributions to the theatre, but little in-depth analysis of their works has been written. Explorations have been made into the plays of some of the modern American playwrights such as Adrienne Kennedy, Megan Terry, Rosalyn Drexler, Rochelle Owens, and Myrna Lamb, but the definitions and judgments drawn have not always been directed toward the goal of integrating the attitudes and philosophy of this "special" group of writers. Nor has there been much discussion of ways in which these women have thought about women in their search for understanding the world, or speculation that women's plays selected from one period of time might shed some perspective on the plays of a past or future period. Each playwright mentioned above has written at least one play which has maintained a substantial audience on a New York stage over a considerable length of time. Considering the importance of these women in their centrality to the American stage, it is surprising that so little attention has been paid them, how little serious analysis, or even tribute, they have received.

According to some contemporary women playwrights, women's works have often been met with biased criticism, unswerving traditionalism, lack of encouragement, and even total disregard. In 1972, Rochelle Owens, author of the avant-garde plays, *Futz, Beclch*, and *Istanbul*, stated that men playwrights of her genre had considerably more opportunity in having their plays critically recognized. Speaking for the Women's Theatre Council, an organization which she and other women playwrights (i. e., Rosalyn Drexler, Maria Irene Fornés, Julie Bovasso, Megan Terry and Adrienne Kennedy) established for the development of a professional theatre, she claimed that in general most of them had been "trivialized and patronized to a great extent."[17] "Any woman," she stated,

> . . . who dares to write in areas of human experience which are considered raw or terrifying or investigative . . . is chastised, disciplined, ridiculed.[18]

Lillian Hellman has stated that theatre critics have been little help in assisting her to find objectivity in her work. In *Pentimento*, she claims that there are not many good critics for any form of art and almost none for the modern theatre. Referring to her successful play, *The Little Foxes*, she pointed out that one critic was blatantly inconsistent, first calling it a "febrile play" and later labelling it "an American classic."[19]

Megan Terry points out that perhaps because of critical disregard her reading public has had a difficult time finding her plays in bookstores and libraries. In her opinion there is an attitude of indifference toward women authors, even toward those whose works have been published.[20]

The writings of several male critics stand as witness to these views. In 1932 the Literary Digest reported that the *New York Morning Telegraph* critic Whitney Bolton, believed that the theatre was rapidly becoming "feminized" in the United States, and this was bad. The playwrights, he claimed, were transforming male characters into "pallid shadows" for the stronger women characters.[21] He cited Rachel Crothers' popularity derived from such plays as *When Ladies Meet, I Loved You Wed, Firebird*, and *Criminal at Large*, which all presented women in dominant roles while men, he complained, served merely as puppets. Bolton contended that an unprecedented reversal had happened: the male qualities of strength, decision, firmness, and control had been seized by women and were out of place in their hands. To him it seemed intolerable to realize the scope of what appeared to be a feminine invasion of an area which had always been masculine territory. He believed, however, that the vogue would not last nor would it continue for he felt that few contemporary women playwrights were "powerful and flawless and strong enough to make the plays stick."[22]

The same point of view was expressed by Norris Houghton, who, in 1947, complained that the theatre had been reduced to "a kind of latter-day female seminary" in which women were the dominating force behind virtually every aspect of the commercial theatre.[23] Male playwrights predominated but they were writing mainly for such actresses as Gertrude Lawrence, Helen Hayes, Ethel Barrymore, and Laurette Taylor; and the popularity of such plays as *The Glass Menagerie, Anna Lucasta, Dream Girl, Joan of Lorraine, I Remember Mama*, and even *Antigone* seemed to be evidence of too much emphasis being placed on women's themes. Houghton expressed the belief that in order for the theatre to serve its artistic ends adequately it must recover its lost sense of masculinity. "Muscularity," "toughness," and "virility" were Houghton's goals which would bring rationality and order back to the theatre.[24]

In what Houghton might have believed to be a tribute to the women of the theatre, he designated Lillian Hellman as the only playwright who seemed capable of confronting successfully the "sinewy and exacting life of our time;" in fact, he added "more successfully than many of her male colleagues."[25]

Earlier, in 1941, George Jean Nathan, critic for *The American Mercury*, had expressed the opinion that women playwrights were generically unable to write as well as men and that this was the reason for their secondary status as dramatists. He ventured three authoritative guesses as to why it appeared that women would never distinguish themselves as playwrights of primary importance. First, he declared, a woman dramatist had seldom succeeded in mastering an economy of emotion. He claimed that a woman playwright tended to stretch an emotion "not only to its extreme limit, but beyond."[26] It was for this reason that he believed most drama written by women resolved itself "willy nilly" into melodrama and that most of their comedy was pushed into the genre of farce; this, he said, was either inherent in women's nature, or was merely a disinclination to hold emotion within bounds. Nevertheless, he surmised that emotional excesses were responsible for the major weaknesses found in women's playwriting. To him, these excesses were the "feminine blind spot" and were suspect in the realm of higher drama.

Secondly, Nathan asserted that it was difficult for a woman to view her characters with objectivity. Although he admitted he had no basis for this belief, he stated that women playwrights in the past had had a difficult time discarding either their personal sympathy for or dislike of the characters they created.[27] For example, the objectivity found by other critics in Clare Boothe's *The Women* he called "careless praise" from the less astute.[28]

Nathan's third belief was that it was almost impossible for a women to present a theme which did not represent a commitment to an absolute right or an absolute wrong. Women writers, he claimed, were incapable of finding a moral middle ground and could not allow for dispute of reason. Their prejudices were transparent and judgments arbitrary, that being the way, he stated, of "ingrained melodramatic emotion."[29]

In similar tones, newspaper columnist Heywood Broun wrote an outraged critique when Clare Boothe's *The Women* was first produced. His attack consisted of accusations that Boothe was vulgarly attempting to degrade the whole human race.[30] Also, Milton Mackaye in his biographical sketch of the same playwright suggested that the idea that Boothe was a social commentator of her time never occurred to her until she read her reviews. In discussing her second successful play, *Kiss the Boys Goodbye*, Mackaye proposed that Boothe was not capable of creating political or sociological scope; once she was made aware of the notion that she could be considered a Left Wing dramatist, he claimed, she was not averse to finding social significance in her own works. He suggested that her own personal animosities directed her writing, not her "economic prescience," and that her characters were nothing more than "spurious identifications."[31]

These examples seem to be what Mary Ellmann calls sex-based opinion, or critical pre-occupation with the fact of the writer's femininity.[32] This perspective from which some male critics have viewed the works of women playwrights seems limiting and perhaps raises the question as to how women themselves have viewed women playwrights in terms of established literary requirements. Specifically, have women critics attempted to encourage writers of their own sex to achieve as artists? Have women critics been cognizant of the particular problems women playwrights face in choosing their themes and drawing their characters as male standards dictate; and have they responded in sympathy with those problems?

The answer to all of these questions, according to Miles, is an emphatic no. There is "a remarkable lack of interest" in the subject of women's work among women writers, she claims.[33] She explains that because the male standard of literary judgment has been accepted as the *only* standard of judgment even the area of criticism has been affected. In her study of the female stereotype in the theatre and motion pictures, *From Reverence to Rape*, Molly Haskell underscores this opinion. She suggests that women critics have not been in the vanguard in dignifying the lot of the female, and that even the most astute of them gravitate instinctively to men and male material, frequently dismissing certain stories as "soap opera" or "women's stories," thus supporting the prejudices of their male colleagues.[34]

It seems a paradox that all of the devices of what Ellmann calls sex-based opinion can be found in the writings of eminent women drama critics. But by accepting as viable the hypothesis that criticism is fashioned after masculine habits of mind, the paradox is not unexpected. Evidence of this assertion can be found in the writings of the few women who are accepted as established theatre critics.

Some effects of male-oriented standards can be explicated from an examination of a 1941 *New York Times Magazine* article written by Charlotte Hughes which presented portraits of the six most popular American women playwrights of the early 1940s. In the article entitled "Women Playmakers," Hughes discussed Lillian Hellman, Clare Boothe, Edna Ferber, Rose Franken, Rachel Crothers, and Zoe Akins as dramatists who had found an unusually prestigious place in the American theatre. Hughes stated that there was nothing remarkable about the fact that these women were enjoying the success that they were and she emphasized the point that none of them expressed any militancy in speaking of making their way as women since, she believed, none of them had ever experienced any difficulties that men had not had as well.[35] From this, it may be supposed that these women, having met traditional requirements, were absorbed easily into the mainstream of the art and were accepted because they wrote like men. The capacity to write, suggested Hughes, was synonymous with the ability to present the conventional image of womanhood, circa 1940; the playwrights as artists, their themes, characterizations, varied styles and material, having nothing to do with the creation of the conventional image, were not discussed.

The judgments of major female critics, more significantly, appear to be governed by the same male criteria. Although women drama critics have been few in number, a fact which by itself seems to warrant study, their views have supported the insidious unwritten law that women writers cannot be studied except in terms of their sex, their capabilities as writers being a secondary consideration.[36]

Specifically, Mary McCarthy, drama critic for *The Partisan Review*, and one of the better-known women writers of both criticism and fiction, often seemed to encourage the acceptance of feminine stereotypes by her attitude toward herself as critic, as well as in her understanding of the works she judged. As a critic she labelled herself "an insufferable little-magazine reviewer" and commented that her "air of supreme authority" was assumed with "few credentials."[37] Her low opinion of herself as a critic is exemplified in her reactions to John Van Druten's play, *The Voice of the Turtle*. Van Druten's work, she wrote, introduced a new American type to the popular stage:

> She is the well-brought-up American girl . . . an innocent, a perennial spinster who will always be more in love with her apartment, her flowers, her possessions, her treasury of quotations from poetry, than with any man . . . This is the eternal college girl, who will be wind-swept and hatless at forty, and whose old age no one so far can predict.[38]

McCarthy praised Van Druten for being honest and observant in recording this character type. His perceptions were insightful and he had presented a light comedy that did not indulge in analysis or satire, she commented. The result, she stated, was that the play could be considered a play exclusively for women, at which women could "smile tenderly and a little fatuously, relaxing happily in self-love as the heroine relaxes in her bath."[39] McCarthy was not offended by the playwright's limited characterization; on the contrary, her contempt was directed toward the proposed prototype. Men, she stated, were out of place in this play; thus the playwright's perspective was not questioned, and McCarthy's denunciation was aimed at her own sex.

Rosamond Gilder, whose reviews were published in *Theatre Arts Magazine* principally during the 1930s and 1940s, was a well-established theatre theoretician who wrote authoritatively of plays produced on Broadway. Generally, her reviews were conservative and expressed what she considered to be the rules of good theatre.

In her writings about women playwrights, Gilder appeared to be searching for obedience to those rules; but often her expectations seemed to vary, and she sometimes expressed inconsistent opinions. In Gilder's view, for example, emotional subplots were not compatible with taut construction; therefore, two plays by Lillian Hellman, *Watch on the Rhine* and *The Searching Wind*, both of which featured these devices, were lesser plays to her. Gilder reviewed *Watch on the Rhine* in 1944 and stated that the play was faulty in structure and was looser in construction than *The Children's Hour* and *The Little Foxes* mainly because of Hellman's emotionalism which, for the critic, bordered on the sentimental. In the case of *The Searching Wind*, in which Hellman made an attempt to explore a love relationship within the main theme of war and the question of political responsibility, Gilder expressed her dislike of the "inept love story" and the "purely sentimental stresses and strains" of the relationship; she suggested that perhaps Hellman was too preoccupied personally with the consequences of world war to recreate the objectivity of her previous work.[40]

But from Rose Franken, love themes were acceptable because Franken usually was able to write "strictly within the confines of the art" while sentimentalizing her stories; this was the discipline which Gilder found in Franken's *Claudia*, and which she praised for "giving more than the usual measure of dramatic satisfaction."[41] In *Claudia*, Franken had found a small field of operation in which to work (a few days in the lives of a girl, her mother, and the girl's husband) and had restricted herself to that field; therefore, Gilder seemed pleased that there was no social significance to the play and no attempt to explain world-shattering problems as there had been in Hellman's *The Searching Wind* and *Watch on the Rhine*. In Gilder's judgment, *Claudia* was not, however, an insignificant domestic drama. The critic praised Franken's sensitivity in depicting her characters' highly-charged emotionality. Franken, she declared, had succeeded in creating personalities who were important and immediate. And her special praise went to the delineation of the character of Claudia even if the "real" qualities which she saw in the character seemed based on the novel eccentricities of female behavior. The processes of Claudia's thought she observed favorably as "daring, discontinuous, illogically logical."[42] Yet Gilder failed to comment on Franken's resolution to her character's immaturity. It would seem that the critic had encouraged the playwright's

adroitness with superficialities but had disregarded the more profound character implications that seemed in need of discussion. The
critic appeared to recognize the urgency in the girl's life to change
but seemed more interested in the erratic and often helpless behavior
of the child-bride.

Nonetheless, Gilder wrote an insightful criticism of one of
Franken's best dramas, *Outrageous Fortune*, in which a variety of
serious themes found in the play was examined. Franken had dealt
with anti-Semitism, homosexuality, marital coldness, and other
"erotic vagaries," all points of argument and conflict which, according to Gilder, the playwright had handled with "a frankness that
permits of no evasion."[43] But, in spite of the playwright's daring in
exposing these social evils, Gilder demanded more concentration on
internal resolution. "She scatters her audience's interest irretriev-
ably," she wrote, concluding that the playwright had failed to resolve the emotional discords which she had originated with such
boldness.[44] Later the critic compared the work to another Franken
drama, *Doctors Disagree*, stating that while the play was dated and
artificial, *Outrageous Fortune* had presented an honest challenge and
inquiry; and although defective dramaturgically, it remained arrest-
ing and memorable.

Euphemia Van Rensselaer Wyatt wrote for *The Catholic
World*, and it is assumed that her views reflected the Church's stand
on moral and ethical issues. Indeed, her writing presented a conservative view of what subjects were suitable for women to explore and
what procedures were acceptable in presenting them. In seeking these
values, Wyatt tended to pass moral judgment on women's works,
evidently valuing instructional possibilities and conventional morality more than individual reaction to experience and feeling. Often
her reviews were didactic digression in which a playwright's themes
were sentimentalized, an archaic use of rhetorical questioning was
affected, and lessons in moral behavior were issued by means of the
work in question. As an example, Wyatt wrote a critique of Rachel
Crothers' successful play, *Let Us Be Gay*, in 1929 but used the discussion as an opportunity to offer her opinion of the playwright's
moral constitution in relation to the techniques of comedy writing.
Consequently, the effectiveness of the play was never analyzed.

Wyatt's digressions continued in later reviews, and often, because of her insistence upon adherence to moral rules, her comments seemed evasive when dealing with women who chose to explore "forbidden" subjects. In her 1935 review of Hellman's *The Children's Hour*, Wyatt was overwhelmed by the playwright's plainly apparent reference to lesbianism but avoided discussing the subject by pointing out that the play touched upon a subject which "we have always felt should be taboo."[45] Again, in 1953, when *The Children's Hour* was revived, Wyatt refused to discuss the situation of the two teachers and commented that "with full loathing, the play touches upon a subject wisely avoided," and she implied that the playwright herself regarded its inclusion as only a necessary evil for plot development.[46]

Similar moral judgment is found in Wyatt's criticism of Rose Franken's *Outrageous Fortune*. To Franken's exposition of themes of homosexuality, prostitution, anti-Semitism, and other problems, Wyatt responded negatively. This was the first time, to her knowledge, that a "harlot . . . is held up as a torchbearer;" and Franken, she felt, had stretched charity to "a very dangerous scuffing of standards" in offering this mixture of tolerance and sentimentality.[47] Clare Boothe's *The Women* was regarded in the same light and all thirty-six women characters who comprised the cast were, in her opinion, irredeemable.[48] Boothe's reliance upon "bad language, prolific wisecracks, and low morals" indicated to Wyatt that the playwright's primary concern was merely to be "popular."[49]

Similarly, Edith J. R. Isaacs, editor for *Theatre Arts Magazine*, indicated that women were in their proper element when they wrote "good and gracious" plays.[50] For Isaacs the disciplined playwright, that is, one who followed the rules of established opinion, was the successful playwright. The light comedies of Rachel Crothers pleased her, particularly *Susan and God*, in which Crothers' theme, technique and characters seemed properly limited. In her review of that work Isaacs commented that the playwright was wise in making her protagonists negligible and the play innocuous. In fact, the play, she said, "never bestrides the serious elements actual or implied."[51]

In more serious drama Isaacs demanded a more tight-knit

formula. She found no redeeming feature in Boothe's *The Women* since it could not be judged according to the structure of the conventional three-act play; in her view it was merely a hodge-podge of feminine deception. In fact,the play might be viewed as a case study of the female sex in which loose minds, loose morals, backbite, "and any other contemptible quality" were expected.[52]

It was Lillian Hellman's apparent single-minded devotion to an idea and her ability to translate the idea into dramatic form that was, for Isaacs, both Hellman's weakness and strength. While Isaacs admired the playwright's powers of persuasion, invention, and technique, she criticized her stubborn determination to go her own way. It was inexplicable to the critic that the playwright should be so convincing in character, plot, and conflict, and yet be so lacking in artistic discipline. She cited *The Children's Hour* as an example. In her opinion even though the play could hold and attract audience attention, the author lost control of her material and let it run where it would.[53] To be convincing, according to Isaacs, the play should have run its own straight and inevitable course; instead "the playwright chose her own rather than the play's indomitable way."[54] In addition, Isaacs believed that Hellman's belligerent morality was unwise and that her technique of dinning a moral into the ears of an audience was too aggressive; in her view the social anger found in all of Hellman's works jeopardized her more disciplined work. Hellman was capable of writing only in categorical blacks and whites, suggested Isaacs, and she could not see situations or characters in larger dimensions. Yet she praised Hellman's plea for an active total goodness contained in a speech of one of the negro characters of *The Little Foxes*.

These four major women critics all seem to be influenced by the predominant critical mode of play analysis. In general they concern themselves with what they regard as certain immutable laws of drama. With a special (perhaps socially directed) inclination toward morality, philosophy, conservatism, and conventionality, the four critics often discuss women playwrights in terms of how they fit into the established art of dramatization. Perhaps much of their material was shaped by the publication for which they were writing (this seems particularly obvious in the case of Euphemia Van

Rensselaer Wyatt who wrote for *The Catholic World* and Mary Mc-Carthy who was drama critic for *The Partisan Review*), nevertheless, their comments seem consistent with the guiding principles set down by traditional (male) standards.

Unfortunately, total allegiance to this kind of criticism emphasizes the predicament that women critics, along with their sister writers, seem alienated from the very source to which they could look for response and to which they could respond. This situation creates inconsistencies in the work of the female critic who unquestioningly subscribes to sex-based judgment. The values therein may produce a complex hostility: a critic may tend to reject the work which does not conform to sexual preconception, that is, if feminine concerns can be found, "they are conventionally rebuked," but, if not, their "absence is shocking;" while all women's writing, Ellmann noted, should presumably strive for a "supra-feminine condition," it is distrusted for achieving it or it is frowned upon for not attempting to achieve it.[55] Thus it seems there has been little written by women critics about women playwrights to mitigate the excesses of sex-based criticism.

Notes

[1]Seymour M. Farber and Roger H. L. Wilson, eds., *The Potential of Woman* (San Francisco: McGraw-Hill Book Company, Inc., 1963), p. vii.

[2]Marya Mannes, "The Problems of Creative Women," in *The Potential of Woman*, ed. by Seymour M. Farber and Roger H. L. Wilson (San Francisco: McGraw-Hill Book Company, Inc., 1963), p. 120.

[3]Michele Murray, ed., *A House of Good Proportion* (New York: Simon & Schuster, 1973), p. 13.

[4]Virginia Woolf, *A Room of One's Own* (New York: Harcourt, Brace & World, Inc., 1929), p. 79.

[5]Murray, *A House of Good Proportion*, pp. 18-19.

[6]Ellen Moers, "The Angry Young Women," in *Harper's Magazine* 227. No. 1363 (December 1963), p. 89.

[7]Mary Ellmann, *Thinking About Women* (New York: Harcourt, Brace & World, Inc., 1968), p. 195.

[8]Louise Bernikow, *The World Split Open* (New York: Vintage Books, a Division of Random House, 1974), p. 6.

[9]Rosalind Miles, *The Fiction of Sex* (London: Vision Press, 1974), p. 39.

[10]*Ibid.*, p. 38.

[11]*Idem.*

[12]Lillian Hellman, *An Unfinished Woman* (Boston: Little, Brown & Company, 1969), pp. 75-76.

[13]Edith J. R. Isaacs, "Lillian Hellman, a Playwright on the March," in *Theatre Arts*, 28 (January 1944), p. 20.

[14]*Idem.*

[15]Miles, *The Fiction of Sex*, p. 38.

[16]*Idem.*

[17]"Five Important Playwrights Talk About Theatre Without Compromise and Sexism," *Mademoiselle*, 75 (August 1972), p. 289.

[18]*Idem.*

[19]Lillian Hellman, *Pentimento: A Book of Portraits* (Boston: Little, Brown & Company, 1973), p. 179.

[20]"Five Important Playwrights Talk About Theatre Without Compromise and Sexism," p. 289.

[21]"Men Fading out of the Play," in *The Literary Digest* (24 December 1932), p. 114.

[22]*Idem.*

[23]Norris Houghton, "It's A Woman's World," in *Theatre Arts*, 31 (January 1947), p. 31.

[24]*Ibid.*, p. 34.

[25]*Idem.*

[26]George Jean Nathan, "Playwrights in Petticoats," in *The American Mercury*, 52 (June 1941), p. 750.

[27]*Idem.*

[28]*Idem.*

[29]*Ibid.*, p. 753.

[30]Milton Mackaye, "Clare Boothe," in *Scribner's Magazine*, 105. No. 3 (March 1939), p. 13.

[31]*Ibid.*, p. 50.

[32]Ellmann, *Thinking About Women*, p. 29.

[33]Miles, *The Fiction of Sex*, p. 22.

[34]Molly Haskell, *From Reverence to Rape* (Baltimore, Maryland: Penguin Books, Inc., 1973), pp. 13-14.

[35]Charlotte Hughes, "Women Playmakers," in The *New York Times Magazine*, 4 May 1941, p. 10.

[36]Miles, *The Fiction of Sex*, p. 21.

[37]Mary McCarthy, *Mary McCarthy's Theatre Chronicles 1937-1962* (New York: Farrar, Straus and Company, 1963), p. xvi.

[38]*Ibid.*, pp. 74-75.

[39]*Idem.*

[40]Rosamond Gilder, "Legitimate Hopes: Broadway in Prospect," in *Theatre Arts*, 28. No. 10 (October 1944), p. 566.

[41]Rosamond Gilder, "When the Earth Quakes," in *Theatre Arts Monthly*, 25. No. 4 (April 1941), p. 262.

[42]*Idem.*

[43]Rosamond Gilder, "Broadway in Review," in *Theatre Arts* 28. No. 1 (January 1944), pp. 8-9.

[44]*Idem.*

[45]Euphemia Van Rensselaer Wyatt, "The Drama," in *The Catholic World*. 140 (January 1935), pp. 466-467.

[46]Euphemia Van Rensselaer Wyatt, "Theatre," in *The Catholic World*, 176 (February 1953), p. 388.

[47]Euphemia Van Rensselaer Wyatt, "The Drama," in *The Catholic World*, 158 (February 1944), p. 488.

[48]*Idem.*

[49]Euphemia Van Rensselaer Wyatt, "The Drama," in *The Catholic World*, 150 (December 1939), p. 339.

[50]Edith J. R. Isaacs, "Broadway in Review," in *Theatre Arts Monthly*, 21. No. 12 (December 1937), p. 917.

[51]*Idem.*

[52]Edith J. R. Isaacs, "Broadway in Review," in *Theatre Arts Monthly*, 21 (February 1937), p. 101.

[53]Edith J. R. Isaacs, "Broadway in Review," in *Theatre Arts Monthly*, 19 (January 1935), p. 13.

[54]*Idem.*

[55]Ellmann, *Thinking About Women*, p. 40.

Chapter II

1930-1940

The primary focus of this study is to investigate the exclusivity of American women playwrights who wrote from 1930 to 1970, to examine their view of women, and to explore the question: have women dramatists been able to define what their characters are, not necessarily through traditional forms and themes, that is, based on traditionally male standards, but on the basis of what has shaped their own lives? In the following chapters a decade-by-decade examination of selected plays will be presented as a background for conclusions and answers to the questions raised.

According to Burns Mantle, a reliable chronicler of the American theatre, the decade from 1930 to 1940 was marked by a series of economic and political disruptions which exerted important influences on the theatre seasons in New York City. Nonetheless, women playwrights contributed several successful plays at that time. Nine plays by women had run at least thirty performances on Broadway stages. Four of the six playwrights responsible for those works, Susan Glaspell, Rose Franken, Zoe Akins, and Rachel Crothers, were already well-established writers prior to 1930. Both Rachel Crothers and Zoe Akins received Pulitzer prizes for plays written during this time, and the first plays of Lillian Hellman and Clare Boothe were produced.

From 1930 to 1932 relatively few comedies were produced on Broadway, and women followed this general trend toward serious drama. Susan Glaspell reflected a tradition of the past in a sentimentalized treatment of an historical figure in her 1930 Pulitzer Prize winning *Alison's House*.

Actress, journalist, novelist, political reporter, and playwright,

Glaspell began her theatrical career in 1919 at the Neighborhood Playhouse and was one of the organizers of the theatre which later became known as the Provincetown Players. This group provided a showcase for several of her works, such as her 1916 play, *Trifles*, which brought her fame. A year later she and her husband, George Cram Cook, wrote a satire on the excesses of psychoanalysis called *Suppressed Desires* which conveyed sardonic wit and imaginative boldness and brought Glaspell recognition as a leading American playwright.[1] Soon her plays were brought to the attention of Eva LeGallienne and her Civic Repertory Theatre. It was there that *Alison's House*, perhaps her most popular play, was first produced December 1, 1930.

Based partly on the life of Emily Dickinson, the play deals with the collapse of family tradition. Alison Stanhope (Emily Dickinson) has been dead for eighteen years. It is New Year's Eve, 1899, and the family is making final arrangements to leave the house in which all of them have lived and in which Alison has died. The attitudes of the new century with its new morality and experience threaten the refinements of the old century, represented by the lingering spirituality of Alison. A strong sub-plot deals with the illicit love affairs of certain family members, principally Elsa, Alison's niece. Upon discovering some long-hidden, intimate poems by Alison, which prove to be her finest, each member is able to resolve personal suffering through the surviving influence of the poet's personality. The poems contain an account of the poet's own confrontation with an illicit relationship which she has relinquished in sacrifice to her family's honor.

Described by critics as a "literary play," meaning that it was "burdened with intelligence, a generally undramatic story and . . . stiff dialogue," *Alison's House* did not enjoy wide popular appeal, and critical reaction was generally polite praising of the moral virtues it propounded.[2] Yet the play was awarded the Pulitzer Prize in 1931 despite strong objections. Many of the reviewers opposed the play's nomination because, in their opinion, it lacked "entertainment value," although the purpose of the award was to recognize the representative original play which had been performed in New York which would best characterize the "educational value and power of the stage."[3]

For Francis Fergusson, drama reviewer for *The Bookman*, the play's atmosphere resembled that of Chekhov's *The Cherry Orchard*, in which traditions of the old century were forced to give way to the vulgarities of the new. Fergusson felt that the play was full of good ideas, albeit derivative of Chekhov, the main one being the device of the family house, dismantled and sold as a vacation resort, to indicate the destruction of a tradition.[4]

The play is indeed one of mood and character wherein everything in the old house is reminiscent of the most important character, the dead Alison, whom Glaspell drew in memory as an extraordinary poet and human being, and from whose spirit an influence of understanding and love continued to be felt. Euphemia Van Rensselaer Wyatt noted that the mood which Glaspell established had captured a sense of the dramatic in inanimate things, such as the old house and the relinquishment of its secrets, and in the spiritual serenity which fills Alison's bedroom where Elsa, Alison's morally liberated niece—the new woman of the twentieth century—reads the secret poems.[5]

In Glaspell's characters an intriguing contrast is drawn between Alison, the spinster-poet who has ennobled the family name with her artistry, and Elsa, the libertine who has brought disgrace to the family by running away to live with a married man. Ironically, Elsa learns that her aunt had faced a love similar to hers but rejected it out of Victorian duty and honor. Having kept it a secret, Alison expressed the anguish of her loss in her last poems. From her aunt's hidden despair, Elsa perceives that in fulfilling her own passion she has found no peace, that she has offered herself as the source of inspiration for one man; but Alison, through self-denial, has remained the source of inspiration for mankind. Alison's virtues seem real to Elsa and more tangible than her own "liberated" way of life which seems empty and artificial by comparison. But Elsa finds acceptance and comfort in Alison's eloquent justification of individual choice, apparently the theme of her poems. From Elsa's standpoint it is Alison, not she, who has found an autonomous definition of her life and ultimately is the more liberated of the two.

Thus the relationship between the two is dominated by one highly abstract idea: the consequences of choice in a moral decision and the acceptance of the responsibilities implicit in the choice made. In the closing scene of the play, even though it is obvious that Alison and Elsa stand at opposite poles of morality in the eyes of society, Glaspell suggests that there is a link that joins the two together. Both have suffered from the consequences of their decisions, Elsa from the awareness of the pain she has brought others and Alison from the despair of loneliness as an unmarried and childless woman. But coincidentally, Alison's justification for her decision has brought to Elsa an understanding of her own actions, and the two share happiness in sorrow in accepting what they felt they had to do. Elsa thinks of the secret poems as Alison's gift, to be given first to her, then to all women, and ultimately, to all mankind.

Rose Franken's *Another Language* was produced the following year. It was similar to *Alison's House* in the topic of family tradition, but presented the dissimilar view that these traditions tended to stultify and rob its members of individuality. Franken's play, although expressing the same domestic dilemma as found in Susan Glaspell's work—the plight of a woman ostracized by her family for unconventional beliefs and behavior—emphasized the positive value of a woman's right to self-assertion in spite of family disapproval.

Another Language was the playwright's first produced play, and it was successful; but it was not Franken's first attmept at playwriting. Other earlier efforts had failed, including a work called *Fortnight* which had been promised production but had never materialized on the stage. Franken was an experienced short-story writer and, after the success of *Another Language*, wrote *Claudia*, first as a series of adventure stories, then as a novel, and finally as a play. *Claudia* was an overwhelming stage success in 1941 and will be discussed in a later chapter.

Coming late in the season and with little financial backing, *Another Language* proved to be "a showman's chance" rewarded—it was an immediate success. It was suspected by some critics that the first night reaction came from a papered house, but most critics found in it a basic honesty which seemed refreshing in comparison to the string of dismal failures on Broadway that had preceded it.

Euphemia Van Renssalaer Wyatt was happy to find it a "real play" in which honesty, humor, "and yet such a delicate psychology" were offered.6 Burns Mantle attributed its success to the fact that its honest achievement in both writing and playing inspired an equally honest reaction upon the part of the theatre patrons. He wrote that the play was successful because it was simple in plot, character and composition. It was, he stated, built firmly on a foundation of human plausibility.7 Mantle described the plot:

> The story has a Candida background in that it tells of a youthful aunt who is the only one of a large family who expresses sympathy with an adolescent boy of artistic ambitions. The boy falls desperately in love with his aunt, but circumstances and her good common sense are equal to a reasonable solution of the resulting problem.8

But this is a superficial examination of what occurs, for Mantle has overlooked the crux of the conflict: the aunt's own frustration and artistic ambitions which form a more important theme, that of a woman's recognition of her unfulfilled needs. Actually, the play centers on Stella, the aunt, and her alienation from a solidly self-righteous and vulgar family. Her dilemma is to choose to be true to her own refined sensibilities or to be drawn in as part of a family made up of dull, mediocre individuals who live the half-lives of the bourgeoisie. Stella attempts to articulate her frustrations to her husband, declaring that she wants more from life than merely waking up in the morning and going to bed at night and the routine of a man and woman living together.9 But Vickie dismisses this as just garden variety romance. Yet it is her devotion to her husband and her concern that he is being slowly engulfed by the family that keeps Stella from leaving. Finally, she does seem to succeed in winning her husband's understanding, thus inspiring in him a desire to shake off the superficial values of his family and to find his own independence.

Another Language was originally called *Hallam Wives*, the surname derived from the family into which the heroine has married; this is evidently an indication that Franken wanted to emphasize the plight of women who by marriage are thrust into an encompassing family situation which tends to discount individuality. Inevitably, a Hallam marriage, rather than broadening the scope of the family, ends up being absorbed into the family mentality which ridicules what it does not understand. This is the conflict which confronts Stella who cannot deny her opposing view of life nor her desire to make a better life for herself and her husband. The conflict is an obvious one: the philistine element vs. the artistic, and it is made more obvious by the details of character. The matriarch of the family, the source from which all family opinion must agree or be excluded, is the personification of practicality and possessiveness. This is contrasted with Stella's love of sculpture and music and her interest in her nephew's discouraged ambition to become an architect. The theme emerges from this conflict as Stella's grievances are finally heard by her husband: ideals can become realities with honest determination.

During the 1934-35 post-depression season, economizing efforts became evident in theatre production. Experimentation in new ways and means of expressing the topics that interested a society in changing times was characteristic. The draining of established New York talent by Hollywood had forced producers to seek and encourage new talent. It was then that a new playwright, Lillian Hellman, emerged. Her first play, *The Children's Hour*, when produced in 1934, attracted attention by its powerfully stated theme and treatment of heretofore "forbidden" subject matter.

Hellman's literary background was established first in other occupations: she was a play reader for Herman Shumlin, who later produced *The Children's Hour*; she spent some time as a book reviewer for the *New York Herald Tribune*; she read film scenarios for Metro-Goldwyn-Mayer in Hollywood and worked as a theatrical press agent; in addition, she regularly contributed stories and articles to magazines and publications. Her first experience as a playwright was as co-author of a farce, *Dear Queen*, which she wrote with Louis Kronenberger, but it was never produced.

Taking her inspiration from a criminal trial fought through the Scottish courts, the case often referred to as the Great Drumsheugh Case in which two women school teachers were accused of an unnatural relationship, Hellman composed *The Children's Hour* as a play of such compelling force that when produced in 1934 it attracted much attention and drew unexpectedly large and continuous audiences.

Interest in the play was aroused by its complex socio-psychological probing. Accepted as a serious and sincere study of abnormal psychology, the play "struck Broadway like a thunderbolt," said Whitney Bolton.[10] Audiences and critics alike were stunned by the undeniable talent and unrelenting strength of the new playwright, as well as the unprecedented subject matter.

The Children's Hour was nominated for the Pulitzer Prize, but even though the judges voted it the outstanding play of six nominated, it was considered too frank in its handling of the subject of lesbianism, which, according to Mantle, produced "a taint of unwholesomeness" that unquestionably had an effect upon a critical estimate of the drama's worth.[11] Indeed, the topic of lesbian love had heretofore been thought of as being confined to the comments of burlesque comedians and the writers of topical revue sketches; thus many critics preferred to overlook the perverse references and to restrict their views to the more conventional central theme, namely, the devastating effects of a lie.[12]

The play opens at the Wright-Dobie school for girls. Karen Wright and Martha Dobie, after several years of struggling to establish the school, finally are realizing some security. Mary, one the students, starts a malicious lie about an unnatural relationship between the two women. The scandal precipitates tragic results: the women lose the school, and their reputations are ruined. Later it is learned that the gossip has been pure fabrication, but the damage has been done. Martha, believing there is some hidden basis of truth in the child's accusation, confesses this to Karen, then shoots herself. Karen secludes herself from the society which has condemned her and which now seeks futile reparation.

Hellman is concerned with the problem of human evils which cause unjust punishment, and attention is brought to this theme on psychological and social levels. The theme is supported by the revelation of the shocking power of gossip and the diseased nature of evil. Society, or the upright people of the world, is disclosed as a foolish group of people, tragically blundering because of its own self-righteousness and ignorance. The ascendance of the wickedness which springs from the lie of the child is weighed against the descending capacity for the truth to survive. With relentless momentum, deception out-balances truth, and the irreparable damage is done to the two main characters.

The Children's Hour considers the relationship between the two feminine characters on social and psychological levels. Once college friends, Karen and Martha are now colleagues in self-made positions of authority. Victoria Sullivan and James Hatch point out that in placing the two women in such positions and by forcing the action against them, Hellman was indicating the point of view and exposing a social prejudice that women in authority have always been vulnerable to slander; for normal women, in society's view, do not seek careers.[13] In this position as victims of a society which can be blinded by implacable evil forces, the characters, emotionally and mentally, take on tragic stature. Supporting this opinion, *The Literary Digest* stated that there had not been in the theatre in years any two characters more tragic than the two teachers whose lives are ruined as a result of the evil brought on by such an unlikely source.[14] Indeed, the two women seem to personify Hellman's view of the hopeless struggles of human beings who contend against evils, as well as the unresolved incompatibilities of human nature, particularly women's nature, with society. Karen wonders if there is any place the two can go to re-establish their lives; Martha responds that there will never be any place for them to go now.

Joseph Wood Krutch called Hellman's view, as typified in Martha and Karen, that part of the common denominator of her style which governed her work. Hellman, he declared, was not a specialist in abnormal psychology, but one in hate and frustration, "a student of helpless rage, an articulator of inarticulate loathings."[15] *The Children's Hour*, he stated, was successful in spite of the "almost universal agreement" that it nearly deserted its own subject in the last act when attention was directed toward the confession of guilt by Martha.[16] This was the most serious defect in the play, he felt, and he concluded that Hellman herself did not know what motivated the power behind her creative ability thus she had not yet discovered where the center of the play actually lay. This was an occasion for her rage, he observed, but was it really a cause?[17] Perhaps the causes for Hellman's rage, the results of which manifest themselves in the characterizations of Martha and Karen, are to be found in the social injustice brought about by the prejudicial and circumstantial evidence which has condemned the two women. The grounds for belief in the allegations are flimsy but nonetheless believed, first by the town, then by friends, and finally by the two women themselves. Martha pronounces a pathetic judgment on herself, basing her conclusion that she is, in fact, "what they said," on the rationale that she has never loved a man (she has always been told that this was "unnatural"), that she is jealous of Karen's fiance, and that she lacks Karen's obvious feminine appeal. Because she accepts these reasons as infallible proof of her guilt, she kills herself. Thus the bleakness and poignancy increases with Hellman's further exploration in the last act into the particular dilemma of the two women. The situation is left unresolved, as it is unresolvable, reflecting as profound a human conflict as the more universal struggle between good and evil which is propounded in the first two acts.

Later in the 1934-35 season, *The Children's Hour* was contrasted by a traditional romantic drama, *The Old Maid*, by Zoe Akins. Expressing a theme dealing with maternal instinct, Akins' strongly sentimental drama, based on a novel by Edith Wharton, met with acceptance and was so esteemed as to win the Pulitzer Prize for that year.

Akins, born in 1886, was a promising poet before gaining recognition as a playwright. In 1919 her first play, *Declassee*, achieved notice as a starring vehicle for Ethel Barrymore. Two other works, *Papa* and *The Magical City*, produced by the Washington Square Players (which later became the Theatre Guild), were introduced the same year. Several more plays followed, including the internationally acclaimed, *The Greeks Had a Word for It*, in 1931. Proficient at adapting and translating foreign works as well as dramatizing novels, Akins achieved more prominence by bringing other important works to the American theatre. Her outstanding accomplishment in the theatre was *The Old Maid*.

Prior to its New York run, *The Old Maid* opened to an invited audience in Baltimore which consisted of an odd mixture of critics and twelve hundred Baltimore matrons. The ladies received the play enthusiastically, but the critics' judgment was not favorable. The majority of the reviewers insisted that the play was too obvious in its sentimentality and that it followed an older form of emotional drama which likely would not satisfy sophisticated playgoers of the day. Indeed, the New York opening was met with reserved and per- functory criticism. But the play gained in reputation, being consider- ed a great "woman's play," and on the strength of its attraction to the matinee audiences, it had a lengthy run. After much divided opinion among the Pulitzer Prize committee of judges, it was desig- nated the outstanding representative American drama for that year.

The scene of the play is set in New York City in 1830 and covers a twenty-year period. The society in which the characters live is stiff and firmly rooted in arid customs and formalities. The drama focuses on two women who throughout this twenty-year period are drawn together by circumstances, familial ties, and a love which they hold in common for one man. Delia, breaking off her relationship with a poor young artist, marries into a proper wealthy family in order to maintain her situation in life and her inheritance. Her cousin, Charlotte, whose circumstances are meager, tells Delia that she has loved the same young artist and has had a child by him. Out of jealousy Delia deceives Charlotte's fiance, thus destroying her cousin's chances of security and happiness. The two women hide Charlotte's indiscretion and raise the child together in Delia's home with Delia assuming the role of the child's mother and Char- lotte the "old maid" aunt. The child grows to womanhood, and on the eve of her wedding, Charlotte and Delia are forced into a final resolution of their resentments which they have held for each other over the years and are joined together by the maternal affection they have for the daughter of the man they both have loved.

The Old Maid is a drama of character whose theme explores an atmosphere and time in which feminine identity could only be sought through the competitive relationship by its two main characters. Living in a society which demands decorum, even if honesty must be sacrificed, Delia and Charlotte are caught in its confines and are forced to sacrifice inner desires to the roles which society has prepared for them. Delia must reject the real love of her life out of fear that it may not lead to a conventional wife-mother future. She frankly admits that she could not bear to be an old maid, nevertheless experiences great loneliness in spite of her secure marriage. Charlotte must refuse marriage altogether for the sake of her illegitimate child, but, being forced to keep her secret, finds little fulfillment in caring for the child as her "old maid" aunt. Yet both have dutifully satisfied the expectations of women in their separate classes which society had dictated. It is a society with a double standard, and the dilemma is expressed in the young Charlotte's despair at being unable to risk telling her fiance of her past, even though she realizes he probably has sewn his own wild oats.

The conflict of the drama is derived not so much from the lapses of time, the consequences of passing years, or even social change, as from the development of the two women in their relationship to each other. Both women share the same sorrow, even though Delia appears to have accomplished the requirements of being an entertaining wife and a vibrant, understanding mother; and Charlotte ultimately succeeds in filling her role by hiding her maternal instincts behind the guise of the conventional family adjunct, the stern spinster aunt. Yet both feel similar inner conflicts. At the outset both are fearful of being "old maids" in a society which is predicated on the idea that a woman alone is an oddity to be tolerated if not despised. Both display a strange subdued brutality toward each other which results, the playwright implies, from superficial standards of decency and convention. They counter-balance each other, one dominating, the other being dominated, both inevitably tied together first by fear of loneliness, then by the realization of the suffering they have caused in one another which gradually makes them aware of their love for and dependence upon each other.

For all the datedness, Akins has drawn a modern study of

women which reveals the characters as more than simplifications of personalities. Stark Young indicated this characteristic as the element of sophistication in the play; that is, the characters "are not all black and white, villainous or beatific, smart or somber."[18] In Delia there is a concentration of reaction to and confusion in both good and bad impulses, conscious and subconscious. Charlotte, the less dominating character, is a portrayal of continuous retreat and advance, an obstinate force frightened by the dread of consequences, yet urged by her own integrity to act. Both characters, from Young's point of view, are "a long way above the usual stage simplification or hollowness."[19]

During the 1936-37 season the American theatre suffered from a shortage of new plays (ninety, as compared with the late 1920s figure of two hundred and sixty). Mantle cited three causes for this situation: (1) withdrawal of Hollywood backing, (2) the absence of East coast capital, and (3) the consequent absence of better playwrights.[20] This was the year of Clare Boothe's devastating satiric drama of the situation of the New York upper class, *The Women*, in which the satire was directed not only against the feminine element, but also against the idle wealth of the society as a whole.

An extreme contrast to Akins' *The Old Maid*, Boothe's *The Women* presented a completely unsentimental treatment of women from another level of New York society, the Park Avenue elite. The author, being a member of that society when she wrote the play, was a socialite iconoclast, first married to the wealthy George T. Brokaw, then to the publisher of *Time* and *Fortune* magazines, Henry R. Luce. Boothe's professional experience up to that point included work as novelist, actress, and editor of the high-society publication *Vanity Fair*. Her career in playwriting began ignominiously, however, with only one of her first four plays being produced, *Abide with Me*, which failed. But her fifth play, *The Women*, a frank satire on the lives of idle, rich women of her own class, was received enthusiastically, particularly by women patrons who, Mantle observed, evidently enjoyed being witness to the exposure of these selected female types.[21]

Needless to say, the play invited an assortment of criticism which was not necessarily concerned with Boothe's abilities as a playwright but with the ostensible condemnation of her sex which she had formulated. But Boothe wrote a preface to *The Women* in which she stated that she harbored no illusions regarding the play as an exposure of her sex or, for that matter, as to its quality as contemporary literature:

> *The Women* is a satirical play about a numerically small group of ladies native to the Park Avenues of America. It was clearly so conceived and patently so executed. The title, which embraces half the human species, is therefore rather too roomy ... its very generality seemed to hold a wide audience appeal, a consideration which few commercial dramatists are required to ignore. This having been frankly stated, I am sure that few readers will be distracted by the width of the title from the narrowness of the play's aim: a clinical study of a more or less isolated group, projected, perhaps in bad temper, but in good faith. The reader, who, warned of this, nevertheless claims to discover in it a portrait of all womankind, is obviously bound to experience the paradoxical discomfort which ensues to the wearer when the shoe unexpectedly fits.[22]

Mary Haines, the major character, is set against a crowd of Park Avenue cynics, slanderers, and backbiters; her attempts to cut through the artifices of this society form the major action of the play. The other characters, being satiric types, represent different aspects of the amoral, unprincipled society of which Mary is a part. Boothe presents an assortment of situations which are connected by contrasting the ingenuousness of Mary with the abnormalities of her peers, these situations forming the structure of the simple plot: Mary learns of her husband's infidelity, seeks a divorce in Reno, gets it, then later, realizing that she still loves him, sets out to win him back using the same feminine strategies employed by her associates.

Thematically it is an exposé of the social tactics of the wealthy and an attack on the shallow, superficial customs and rituals which direct that society. In the view of Sullivan and Hatch, the work is, and yet is not, an expression of hatred for the female sex. In the dialogue and characterizations it appears to be. One character, speaking of her pregnancy, states that girls always make one sicker.

Another, a writer, had just completed a book for which, she says, her female readers have been waiting, entitled *All the Dead Ladies*. It is about all the women she dislikes. Miriam, the cynical musical comedy star, advises Mary to resolve her marital problems by compromising. In her opinion, Miriam consoles, a woman is compromised the day she is born. From these and other similar pieces of advice Mary learns how to understand other women by not trusting them.

It seems clear that in none of the characters of *The Women* does the playwright make a positive assessment of the female sex. In fact, all of the women, from Mary's twelve year old daughter to the dowager Countess, are pictured as trivial, predatory, and insecure. Milton Mackaye concluded that Boothe presented no important character with whom she herself was sympathetic, and in fact, he commented, the playwright even regarded Mary, the ostensible heroine, as "a fathead."[23]

The caricatured world of Clare Boothe is full of malicious and brutalizing portraits. Yet some scholars have attempted to define her characterizations by disregarding the question of her sex disloyalty and have compared her style with that of the Restoration writers Congreve, Wycherley, and Farquhar. The comparison is not an idle one, for there can be found the same elements: "the aridity of emotion," a "scabrous comedy of manners," and an "outrageous cartooning of human frailty."[24] Indeed, the thirty-six women who make up the cast of characters are outlined by the kind of pessimistic satire found in Restoration comedy. As they move through their smart, sophisticated, yet heartless social circles, they function as the personifications of Boothe's theme. In this way the playwright is not totally condemning her sex; she poses a legitimate question as to the validity of the belief that all a woman has to offer a man is sex. By showing these women at their worst, Boothe challenges them to reveal their best. This is indicated in Mary's struggle to define and support herself on the basis of her own personal convictions.

Interestingly, despite the seeming independence of this free-wheeling feminine society and no matter how vehemently the suspicions of the opposite sex are expressed, the women are totally defined by their relationships to their men, although no male character ever appears. In Boothe's view there are few alternative ways in which these women can define themselves. For them, the one tragedy in their lives is to lose their men. A reverse lifestyle, that is, living alone without male support, and liking it, is inconceivable since all values are materialistic; and since men are the suppliers of the commodities of wealth, comfort, and pleasure, they must be regarded as necessary evils. Nancy, the socialite-writer whose work is less than profound, is a virgin and, with ironic coincidence, is also the only woman of her set who supports herself. Yet, "I'm what nature abhors," she says ". . . a frozen asset."[25] Another character, the dubious Countess, dreamily justifies her past: "What else can a woman do with her youth but give it to a man?"[26] The same philosophy is echoed in the comments of the middle-class women who work in the exclusive dress shop where Mary meets her competition, Crystal. Observing Crystal's shapely figure, a fitter exclaims:

> 1st Saleswoman: Look at that body. She's got him now.
> 2nd Saleswoman: You can't trust any man. *That's* all they want.
> Corset Model: (Plaintively, her hands on her lovely hips.) What else have we got to give?[27]

And Stephen Haines' office worker says:

> I wish I could get a man to foot my bills. I'm sick and tired of cooking my own breakfast, sloshing through the rain at 8 a. m., working like a dog. For what? Independence? A lot of independence you have on a woman's wages. I'd shuck it like that for a decent, or indecent, home.[28]

Boothe wrote two other minor successes during this decade, both of which displayed the same satiric thrust as *The Women*, but both less sensational in effect. *Kiss the Boys Goodbye*, produced in 1938, was a scathing farce. This time the playwright satirized Hollywood, big business, and the publishing world. The following year Boothe wrote *Margin for Error*, turning her powers of satire on the encroaching situation of Nazism. Neither play was an overwhelming success as *The Women* was, but both were substantial enough for critics to concede that in writing them the author had discovered the "proper vent for her keenest satire."[29]

The next season, 1937-38, was mainly a novel and experimental season in spite of financial restrictions and capital depletion from West coast sources. Again the frivolities of the idle rich were criticized, this time from the gentler hand of Rachel Crothers in her play *Susan and God*.

Rachel Crothers, considered at one time to be the "leader of our native lady playwrights," often explored symptoms of failure in American society.[30] She devoted much attention to domestic and marital problems, and, in fact, began writing as "something of a radical feminist" as far back as 1904 with one of her first works, *The Point of View*.[31] She continued writing, acting, and directing her own works successfully for the next thirty years. Her first notable achievement was in 1909 with *A Man's World*, in which she explored the situation of the suppression of women in a patriarchal society. She treated the confusions of separation and divorce in three works, *Let Us Be Gay*, *As Husbands Go*, and *When Ladies Meet*, all three popular plays prior to 1930. Often critics viewed Crothers' works as "a long procession reflecting a changing attitude toward women"; the playwright responded that, if this were true, it was an unconscious reaction on her part toward what had been happening in life.[32] In any case, the kind of material that attracted her indicated her concern with women's problems. She admitted to calling upon "the way-deep-down insides of women," more than of men, in drawing her central characters who, coincidentally, were predominantly female.[33] In 1937 Crothers' last successful and perhaps most popular play was produced, *Susan and God*.

Brooks Atkinson summed up a general impression of her focus of attention: a current fad for subject material would become a refreshing play in her hands, he stated.[34] To be sure, her plays were remarkably current in treating the rapid changes of manners which took place during the period in which she wrote (1904-1937) and her adaptability to social change was a characteristic trait.

This flexibility was evident in *Susan and God*, for which Crothers took aspects from the new confessional religious movement in England, the Oxford Movement, and shaped them around her main character as the basis for the plot of her play. The flighty, rich

Susan, having just returned from a trip abroad, comes home to preach to her equally idle friends a new-found religiosity which she has frivolously embraced. Her husband, a near alcoholic, challenges her to practice what she preaches, to help him recover and to bring their unhappy, neglected teen-aged daughter from boarding school to live with them for the summer. Susan reluctantly accepts the challenge and by the end of the summer realizes that her family's needs are of greater importance than her foolish and hypocritical quest to save the world.

Crothers indicates a theme of the universal values of humility, integrity, and service to others, which develops from individual discovery of the importance of those values. Through the objective portrayal of her characters' good and evil impulses, their struggles with wisdom and folly, she proposes that human beings are frail, but can be reclaimed, as Susan and her family have been, through honest self-examination and sincere conversion to true Christian ethics.

Through characterization Crothers reveals that one of her main concerns is for the situation of women in a society which asks few sacrifices and makes fewer demands. Her women characters dominate the action, and even though they are bright, active women with little of the destructive snobbishness of Clare Boothe's figures, they attempt to alleviate the boredom of their lives by pursuing goals similar to those of the Park Avenue set. But Crothers' women are able to resolve their separate predicaments because they become aware that they are ultimately responsible for the choices they make and that the rightness or wrongness of those choices is of their own devising. Irene, Susan's spoiled friend, wants the security of marriage, but evades its responsibilities, justifying her pre-marital relationship by its comfortableness and non-commitment. When Susan interferes and Irene's lover marries someone else, Irene faces her evasion and concludes that it has been her own chosen lifestyle, not Susan's meddling, that has brought about her loss. Charlotte, an attractive spinster who has schemed to seduce Susan's husband, passes up an obvious chance to do so, finally realizing that such an action would violate her own integrity. Leonora, the actress, having given up her career for a marriage of comfort and wealth, finally realizes she is

useless and bored as a wife and returns to the less financially reward-
ing work which nevertheless fulfills her.

The situations of these minor characters are a reflection of the
search for meaning in the vacant life of Susan herself. She, like her
friends, is caught in the dilemma of confused values. Her acceptance
of the new religious cult is a manifestation of her unfocused quest
for life's purpose and "finding God" is just another pastime. Her
true conversion is brought about by a gradual awareness of being
needed and feeling the need for a living relationship with her husband and daughter. In fact, it is not religion at all which has convert-
ed her, but the integrity she has inadvertently inspired in her hapless husband who has derived a sense of purpose and dignity from
being with her. What begins as a superficial diversion ends as a
means by which Susan may be able to face the emptiness of her
relationships and find her true salvation from within.

Toward the close of the 1938-39 period themes of patriotism
as well as criticism of national character were indicated in which
playwrights were expressing their national and racial consciousnesses. Lillian Hellman's *The Little Foxes* pointed to internal social
stresses in the South, made manifest in the domestic machinations
of the infamous Hubbard family. *The Little Foxes* was Hellman's
third play and was received with much the same enthusiasm as her
first, *The Children's Hour. The Little Foxes* won the Drama Critics'
Circle Award as the best play of the year by an American author.

Considered to be the most talked-of drama of the season, *The
Little Foxes* was described by Richard Watts, Jr., of the *New York
Herald Tribune*, as "a psychological horror story."[35] Even more than
that, Hellman created a parable out of the rapacious Hubbard family
who, like "the little foxes that destroy the vines while the vineyards flourish," menace the vineyards of the world by preying upon
society while they rip and tear at each other.[36] The parable, as
Euphemia Van Rensselaer Wyatt noted, is directed towards those
who watch the little foxes at their work but who do nothing to
stop them. This is the theme of the play.

The Little Foxes is a study in avarice which reveals the

machinations of the prosperous Hubbard brothers to steal money to further their industrial empire from their ailing brother-in-law. Through blackmail, deception, and manipulation, Regina reaches her position of power. Refusing to assist her husband when he suffers from a heart attack, she allows him to die, thus securing her position as family despot.

Hellman intended that this play should be "an angry comedy" mixed with drama: "I had not meant people to think of them [the characters] as villains to whom they had no connections," she explained.[37] But the play exceeded her intentions, as evidenced by the domination of her main character. In the figure of Regina the playwright presented a case study of a woman possessed by the forces of ambition which so distort her personality that she has been considered one of the most formidable women characters in the history of American drama. An interesting fact about the development of this character was that she was molded from real life. The real Regina, one of Hellman's mother's ancestors, whose husband died of syphilis, "would speak with outrage of her betrayal by a man (her husband) she had never liked and then would burst out laughing at what she said," Hellman recalled; and, on the day her husband died, the woman dropped the moral complaints forever and went horseback riding during his funeral.[38]

Hellman's dramatized reflection is dominated by one idea: to possess the power, through money, to surpass what she feels is the middle-class mediocrity of her life, symbolized by her drive to be accepted by such a society as Chicago's elite. In fact, she coldly confesses to her husband that her prime reason for marrying him was out of loneliness, not for his companionship, but for the things she never had as a child and felt she was never going to get as a woman alone. She wanted "the world" and, because her brothers had inherited the family wealth, she attempted to secure her position by marriage.

Because she is driven by one force, all traces of what her unscrupulous brother, Ben, calls "the softness of women" are gone. She has so effectively adopted the ways of Ben's double-dealing, unprincipled world and its manners that even he is no match for her.

With her husband in the throes of a fatal heart attack, Regina deliberately exposes her full contempt for him. Demonstrating a blood-chilling composure as she watches him die, she tells him:

> I told you I married you for something. It turned out it was only
> for this. This wasn't what I wanted, but it was something. I never
> thought about it much but if I had I'd have known that you
> would die before I would. But I couldn't have known that you
> would get heart trouble so early and so bad. I'm lucky, Horace.
> I've always been lucky. (Horace turns slowly to the medicine.)
> I'll be lucky again. (Horace reaches for the medicine . . . the
> bottle slips and smashes on the table. He draws in his breath,
> gasps . . . Regina does not move . . .)[39]

Regina's evil solicits the evil of her brothers and their morbid alliance is a stronger force than the weak forces of good found in Horace, her husband, or Birdie, the faded aristocratic sister-in-law. Indeed, Horace is ultimately eliminated; and Birdie, who clings to a memory of kindness and gentility, wanders aimlessly in an inebriated fantasy. Only Alexandra, Regina's daughter, finds a means of retaliation and this must be in escape.

Birdie represents everything that Regina loathes; she is a symbol of an effete, dying Southern aristocracy which is unadaptable to progress and change. Hellman stated that she meant people to smile at the sad, weak Birdie, not to have them cry at her.[40] But the charm and dignity of the character elicits something more than humor and sympathetic reaction. The delicacy of her character is the antithesis of the hard edges of Regina's, and she serves to indicate how far Regina's ambition has carried her.

Notes

[1]John Hutchens, "Broadway in Review," *Theatre Arts Monthly* XV (February 1931), p. 96.

[2]Burns Mantle, *The Best Plays of 1930-31* (New York: Dodd, Mead and Company, 1931), p. 223.

[3]*Ibid.*, p. 222.

[4]Francis Fergusson, "The Theatre: Understanding Recent Openings," *The Bookman* 72 (January 1931), p. 514.

[5]Euphemia Van Rensselaer Wyatt, "The Drama: Plays of Some Importance," *The Catholic World*, 132 (February 1931), p. 591.

[6]Euphemia Van Rensselaer Wyatt, "The Drama: The Theatre Weathers Depression," *The Catholic World*, 135 (July 1932), p. 336.

[7]Burns Mantle, *The Best Plays of 1931-32* (New York: Dodd, Mead and Company, 1932), p. 267.

[8]*Ibid.*, p. viii.

[9]Rose Franken, *Another Language* (Los Angeles: Samuel French, 1932), act 2, p. 71.

[10]Burns Mantle, *The Best Plays of 1934-35* (New York: Dodd, Mead and Company, 1935), p. 33.

[11]*Ibid.*, pp. vi-vii.

[12]*Idem.*

[13]Victoria Sullivan and James Hatch, eds., *Plays By and About Women* (New York: Random House, 1973), p. ix.

[14]"The Thunderbolt of Broadway," *The Literary Digest* 188 (1 December 1934), p. 20.

[15]Joseph Wood Krutch, "Plays, Pleasant and Unpleasant," *The Nation* 143 (26 December 1936), p. 769.

[16]*Idem.*

[17]*Ibid.*, p. 770.

[18]Stark Young, "The Old Maid," *The New Republic* 82 (20 March 1935), p. 162.

[19]*Idem.*

[20]Burns Mantle, *The Best Plays of 1936-37* (New York: Dodd, Mead and Company, 1937), p. 1.

[21]*Ibid.*, p. 219.

[22]*Ibid.*, p. 218.

[23]Milton Mackaye, "Clare Boothe," *Scribner's Magazine* 105 (March 1939), p. 13.

[24]*Idem.*

[25]Clare Boothe, "The Women," in *Plays By and About Women* (New York: Random House, 1973), act 1, sc. 1, p. 105.

[26]*Ibid.*, act 2, sc. 2, p. 165.

[27]*Ibid.*, act 1, sc. 4, p. 136.

[28]*Ibid.*, act 1, sc. 7, p. 153.

[29]Burns Mantle, *The Best Plays of 1939-40* (New York: Dodd, Mead and Company, 1940), p. 317.

[30]Burns Mantle, *The Best Plays of 1937-38* (New York: Dodd, Mead and Company, 1938), p. 199.

[31]*Idem.*

[32]Charlotte Hughes, "Women Playmakers," *New York Times Magazine*, (4 May 1941), p. 27.

[33]*Idem.*

[34]Mantle, *Best Plays 1937-38*, p. 199.

[35]Burns Mantle, *The Best Plays of 1938-39* (New York: Dodd, Mead and Company, 1939), p. 76.

[36]Euphemia Van Rensselaer Wyatt, "The Drama," *The Catholic World* 149 (April 1939), p. 87.

[37]Lillian Hellman, *Pentimento: A Book of Portraits* (Boston: Little, Brown and Company, 1973), p. 180.

[38]*Idem.*

[39]Lillian Hellman, *The Little Foxes* (New York: The Viking Press, 1973), act 3, p. 125.

[40]Hellman, *Pentimento Portraits*, p. 180.

Chapter III

1940-1950

Henry Hewes, an editor of the *Famous American Plays* series, surveyed the general situation of the American theatre in the 1940s and concluded that an evolution had taken place, beginning with the "too carefree" attitude of the 1930s and culminating in the "too careful" period which had developed by 1949 as a result of world war and post-war economics.[1] Hewes noted that perhaps pre-war theatregoers had resented anything that disrupted their idealized picture of life; and, in drama, the public had wanted to be comforted, not disturbed. Before American involvement in World War II there was a general vague awareness of danger to the United States in the struggle among world governments. This half-recognition, to some degree, sponsored a reawakening of ideals, and the philosophy emerged that the danger could be met, it seemed, by good people living and trusting in the principles of democracy. However, after Pearl Harbor the horrors of war demanded a more realistic outlook, and the national attitude was changed by the attempts made to accept the unpleasant task of war while looking to a better future.

Playwrights were challenged by these new demands, and perhaps it was Lillian Hellman's 1941 drama *Watch on the Rhine* which promoted a more down-to-earth perspective among playwrights, a view of the world situation as a tangible threat to the democratic system of government in the United States. In the play Hellman met the challenge with a declaration and defense of American beliefs and values. Setting the pace for several anti-fascist plays to come, the playwright pronounced prophetically that the dangers of fascism were closer to the American society than it seemed to be aware.

Produced in April, 1941, *Watch on the Rhine* was regarded as an "overnight success," perhaps because, as Mantle stated, of all the anti-Nazi dramas that had sprung forth in the past few months, Hellman's was at once "the most soberly reasoned and most convincingly written of the lot."[2] Emotionally moving, yet decisive in its point-of-view, the play brought the prospect of war close to home by evoking sympathy for the victims of the Nazi movement in Europe and, as Gassner observed, by implying that America could not remain neutral for very much longer in the struggle against fascism.[3]

The first showing of the drama was cheered by audiences and lauded by critics. It was awarded the Drama Critics' Circle Award as "a vital, eloquent and compassionate play."[4] Wyatt called its success "a gallant one."[5] And Louis Kronenberger, reviewer for the daily paper, *PM*, wrote that the theatre had found an authoritative voice which made up for all the "waste and blundering and triviality" that he felt was weakening and discrediting the stage at that time.[6]

Hellman sets the play in a suburb of Washington, D. C., in late spring, 1940. Kurt Mueller, an anti-fascist and a central figure in the anti-Nazi underground movement in Europe, has brought his family to his American-born wife's family home ostensibly to establish himself as a German refugee and find work as an engineer for the duration of the war in Europe. The Mueller family has been living poorly from one place to another, and now Sara, Kurt's wife and daughter of the proud and privileged dowager, Fanny Farrelly, anticipates some respite in her mother's home. But also visiting the Farrellys are Teck De Brancovis, an impoverished, opportunistic Romanian count and his wife, Marthe. De Brancovis discovers Mueller's real identity as an underground leader and his intentions to return to Germany to assist the failing movement; he attempts to blackmail Mueller, knowing he is on Hitler's "wanted list." Mueller learns of De Brancovis' scheme which would keep him from going back. Regarding the future of his people as an outweighing factor, Mueller kills De Brancovis, leaves his family in the care of the confused but supportive Fanny, and departs for Germany, knowing he may never return.

As Kronenberger pointed out in his review, the drama does not end as an advocacy for militantism; its strength is found in its deeply human and moving philosophy expressed by Kurt in his farewell to his children in which he declares that all violence is evil, including his own act of murder, but that they will have hope for a better life because of the efforts of men who believe as he believes in a free and orderly world.

The women of the play uphold Kurt's belief in human freedom. Sara, his long-suffering expatriate wife, shares her husband's values, in spite of her longing for the amenities and security she knew as a child with her affluent family. Her life with Kurt is filled with love, but she is not without the bitterness of one who recognizes the inequities suffered by his people. "We live modestly and happily," she explains to her mother, but adds, "as happily as people could in a starved Germany that was going to pieces."[7] Yet she would not change her life. Her decision to sustain Kurt has been based on her own values. She seems justifiably intolerant of the polite political conversation of Teck, the renegade Romanian, and challenges those around her, including her mother, to have their own convictions, to "know where we are and what we have to do."[8] She demonstrates her own belief in what she says when she accepts Kurt's decision to go back to Germany alone, knowing she will never see him again. But she has seen the suffering of a nation and she feels her individual loneliness is nothing compared to what Kurt's efforts may mean to the underground fight for freedom.

Sara's nobility is equal to her husband's and its matched by her mother's effort to understand and help. Kronenberger noted that the play gained in integrity by the inclusion of "the salty, officious great lady" character in Hellman's Fanny Farrelly.[9] As a "sharp-tongued dowager, born to the great world" and a "high-handed representative of the old school," Fanny finds it difficult to understand her daughter's way of life, but she does understand that the Muellers' values are akin to her own.[10] She recognizes that Sara and Kurt are fighting for the dignity of mankind and philosophizes that dignity cannot be put into a man, but if the quality is already there that man can be trusted. The character of Fanny Farrelly provides support to Hellman's own sense of justice which she defined in her memoirs:

> I am ... bewildered by all injustice, at first certain that it
> cannot be, then shocked into rigidity, then obsessed, and fin-
> ally as certain as a Grand Inquisitor that God wishes me to
> move ahead, correctly and holily.[11]

Another play of the 1940-41 season, contrasting Hellman's political orientation, was Rose Franken's *Claudia*. This work reflected the author's facility with domestic drama; it was considered by Mantle as one of the best "lightweight" plays of the season. Franken had left New York for a writing career in California after her play, *Another Language*, achieved success in the early 1930s. She did not return until after her two popular novels, *Claudia* and *Claudia and David*, were published and it was suggested to her that they might be adaptable for the stage. From them the play *Claudia* emerged and was produced. It subsequently was labelled as pleasant escapist drama in which the two main characters, Claudia and David Naughton, were presented as a likeable couple faced with ordinary family problems. Apparently the play was especially appealing to women audiences, a fact attributable, concluded Mantle, to certain "familiar feminine characteristics" of its heroine, Claudia, they being a curiosity regarding her own sex appeal, a "definite mother fixation," and a reluctance to accept full responsibility as a wife.[12]

Franken herself directed the play, and Rosamond Gilder took note of the mood and style which dominated the production and evidently reiterated Franken's purpose of understating pace, movement and accent in order to emphasize the theme of the inherent dignity and nobility of human nature.[13]

Franken's characteristic easy wit and emphasis on the importance of small living experiences were most evident in this play. She traces the pattern of a young girl's immaturity in her inability to accept the responsibilities of marriage and her dependence upon her mother. In the process of the simple plot Franken stresses the theme of the inevitability of life and death and the capacity of human beings to accept these processes with maturity and dignity.

David Naughton, an architect, and his young wife, Claudia, have settled on a farm outside the city. Their happiness is marred by one conflict in Claudia, her obsession to keep her mother with them as much as possible. Neither the mother nor the husband approve of Claudia's reluctance to let her mother go, and, when David learns of the mother's fatal illness, the problem is complicated by Claudia's inability to realize final separation from her. Eventually, and with the realization of her approaching motherhood, Claudia learns to accept the separation and acknowledge her responsibilities as an adult.

The structure of Franken's play rests mainly on character relationships, Claudia being the central figure on whom the action focuses. *Time* magazine referred to the play as a study in "adult infantilism."[13a] Actually, Claudia represents a critical point of development in a woman's life, the gradual awakening to maturity for which, the playwright implies, few women are prepared and many are expected to achieve instantaneously. Claudia's problem is based in her oblivion to the subtleties and complexities of adult life. Her juvenile naivety, evidenced, for example, in her candid reactions to her amorous neighbor, is not a pose but is a result of her ingenousness. When she learns of her pregnancy and, at the same time, of her mother's fatal illness, she faces the ultimate truth that nothing and no one really belongs to anyone.[14] Claudia's entry into adulthood is obtainable only through adult suffering, and she reaches a crossroad in her development when these two important events happen in her life simultaneously. Her youthful illusion that life stands still at its happiest moments is shattered. The strength of her love for her mother is that which enables her to find and follow a path which least resists cruelties. For her mother's sake she perseveres; and, in the process, she is able to accept the realities of human existence, thus fortifying her entrance into the adult world.

The 1941-42 season was a disappointment to the critics, and no prizes were given by either the Drama Critics Circle or the Pulitzer Prize committees. But, according to Mantle, as a "people's" season, it was an intelligent and entertaining year.[15] It marked, however, an especially low point in the production and success of women's plays. This was not necessarily an isolated problem. The situation appeared to be a reflection of the state of material deprivation which the country as a whole suffered during the first two years of the war, as well as a result of the enlistment of man- and womanpower in the initial call for assistance with the war effort.

Sophie Treadwell, still concerned with the economic failures of the past decade, offered *Hope for a Harvest* as the only sustaining play to be written by a woman for that year. Even that ran for only thirty-seven performances.

In 1928 one of the outstanding productions of the Broadway season had been Treadwell's *Machinal*, in which the playwright wrote of a suffering woman caught between a mechanized society and an empty marriage. In the years following, Treadwell devoted most of her time to writing stories and scenarios in California, her native state, and to an acting career which led her into summer stock and vaudeville. She had been a protégée of Helen Modjeska and had assisted the prominent actress in compiling her memoirs. In 1942 Treadwell returned to playwriting, evidently still involved with the concerns of American women who were now facing the effects of war. Concerned with the deterioration of national character and natural resources during a time of crisis, Treadwell explored the general impact this situation had on people, and in particular, women, when she wrote her second, but less successful drama, *Hope for a Harvest*.

The play was called a failure by most critics. It was generally agreed that it was purposeful drama depicting a definite American problem and that Treadwell was sincere in the presentation of the theme; but most reviewers found it dramatically unexciting mainly due to the inclusion of the personal struggles of its main characters.[16] The remarks of Richard Watts, Jr., of the *Herald Tribune*, were typical of the kind of critical response the play received in crediting the playwright's seriousness but disclaiming the play's theatrical value:

> [The play] is really striving to speak to the soul of America with gravity and idealistic fervor. The unfortunate thing is that in expressing the author's heartfelt interest in the future of the nation in a time of desperate crisis the play goes in for some unpersuasive and undramatic theatrical matters which destroy the greater part of its effectiveness.[17]

Mantle suggested that perhaps the cause of Treadwell's "failure" was that, in pattern, the play belonged to the unsophisticated genre of simple folk drama that had flourished twenty or thirty years before, when "experts were fewer and audiences were larger":

> It has its scenes of drama, frequently flaring into touches of melodrama, alternating with scenes of comic relief provided by character types common to the native drama. It even revels in an old-fashioned happy ending that ties up loose ends, loose characters and loose emotions.[18]

The scene is set in the San Joaquin Valley in California during the early months of World War II. Elliott Martin, once a prosperous peach farmer, is now a gas station owner who lives with his sixteen-year old daughter and his mother in their worn down, thirty-year old house. Elliott has become an embittered and prejudiced man since the influx of Italian and Japanese immigrants. His daughter, Tonie, whose mother has died, is anxious to become an aviator and leave the depressing life she leads as her father's gas station attendant. She has been forbidden a relationship with Victor, the son of a prosperous Italian family, who has been sent away to school against his will by his father. In Victor's absence, however, Tonie has carried on an illicit affair with a ne'er-do-well youth whom she does not love but by whom she has become pregnant. Carlotta Thatcher returns after twenty years of living abroad with her husband who is now dead. She and Elliott had grown up together and share many memories, but, as Carlotta is hopeful of making her homestead prosperous again, Elliott refuses to believe that, even by joining forces, they could ever return the wornout, neglected land to its original productive state. But Carlotta, weary of her loneliness and the fears she experienced while living in Europe, cannot be persuaded that the idea is foolish. She instigates actions which join Victor and Tonie together, resolve the prejudices of Elliott and Victor's father, and regenerates the promise of a new life for herself and Elliott.

Treadwell's drama is one of ideas rather than character or plot, and her theme is directed toward the search for the redemption of a social order whose preoccupation with war has deprived its members of their values and dignity. For Rosamond Gilder, who appreciated the play's emphasis on ideas in a time when the theatre seemed to be offering a continuous fare of musical farces, nonsense, and light comedies, Treadwell posed some sound questions about mechanized society vs. landowning and developing and gave these questions valid dramatic form through her characters. Indeed, Treadwell's hope for renewal of life is centered in Carlotta, and, in a symbolic sense, the author has made her the representative of the barren, despoiled land which has been deprived of life by neglect and misdirection. From Treadwell's description, Carlotta is no longer a young woman, but possesses a nervous intensity which gives her personality a youthful appeal. She returns to her childhood home, tired and sick, but with the hope that this place will make her well again. Her illusions of returning to the security and prosperity of America are jeopardized immediately by the conditions under which the family has been living for the last several years, as well as the racial prejudices that exist between the valley natives and the several races of people who have settled there. Both are circumstances from which she hoped to escape when she left Europe. Her fears have been consuming her energy, the fear of being alone, of growing old alone, of being poor. The theme of the play is expressed in her desire to get back to the valley where she will find hope for a more productive life.

Carlotta's efforts to renew her own life extend into the lives of others. She is able to influence the wayward Tonie and help her find a solution to her unhappy situation. She is able to provide employment for the migrant workers who drift in and out of the valley. Her business dealings with the head of the Italian clan are beneficial to both him and herself, even though she humiliates Elliott by dealing with a "dago." And gradually she breaks down Elliott's prejudices about his own failures and inspires in him a renewed faith in life.

When, by the 1943-44 season, the tide of the war had turned, the critical problem of service men returning home and the anticipation of post-war conditions became priority considerations; again playwrights were challenged to explore these new situations. Women playwrights responded by considering the social effects of world conflict and the resulting recuperation. Lillian Hellman wrote *The Searching Wind*, in which she utilized the troubled European scene as background for the personal adjustments involving two women and a man.

Not considered one of her best plays, *The Searching Wind* was, however, regarded as at least "moderately satisfying" and "much the best serious drama to be produced that season."[19] Like *Watch on the Rhine*, it presented strong thoughts on a vital theme which indicated Hellman's impatience with escapist literature and her idea that in a time of crisis the theatre's function went beyond "coddling amatory neuroses."[20] Kronenberger admired her use of the drama as a social tool and applauded her incisive and provocative ideas, her political awareness, and the force of her personality in this work.[21]

In this exposure of the evils of appeasement prior to the Second World War, Hellman hinted that diplomats did as much to bring about the war in their surreptitious efforts to placate the fascist uprising as the fascists did in outright attack.

On another level, Hellman pointed out that the generation of people who had reached middle-age by 1940, were ignorant, frivolous individuals who had created an overwhelming situation and then had handed it over to the younger generation to resolve on the battlefield. She particularized this in the young crippled soldier, Sam, who loses his closest friends while fighting. He is shamed by his parents' attitude that Europe will be liberated when it is restored as the charming, careless, carefree place they once knew.

In flashback scenes the personal and public lives of three individuals are revealed. Played before the background of European conflict, the restive triangular relationship of a young diplomat and two young girls reflects the muddled political scene over a twenty-year period. Eventually Alex, the diplomat, becomes an ambassador, one of the girls becomes his wife, and the other his mistress. The climax of the relationship comes on an evening in 1944 when the wife, Emily, forces a confrontation with the other two.

Cassie, the ambassador's mistress, represents the confusion of their age. Earlier, during the Mussolini takeover in Italy, she has told the young Alex, who, at the time, is the assistant to the Italian ambassador, that she disagrees with his kind of diplomacy. She equates Alex's allegiance to pacifism with their disintegrating personal relationship which was leading to marriage and points out that they are both members of an oblivious generation which sees much but knows very little. She predicts their eventual disillusionment as they move through life unaware of social and political expediencies. To be sure, later, as the United States' ambassador in Paris during the city's evacuation in 1938, Alex recommends appeasement regarding Hitler's aggression in an attempt to prevent involvement. But inevitably world war ensues, and in his own family, his son suffers great losses. Although he has considered it a blameless diplomatic manuever, Alex has made a fatal mistake which he recognizes only years later.

The love story underscores the historical affairs and can be seen as a parable. Stark Young summarized what he thought Hellman was attempting to do: just as the three characters have evaded the realities of their lives, he determined, so have the people of the modern world refused to face the implications and necessities of the final issue, moral involvement in the affairs of men. Lost to an unenlightened generation is the "splendid passion and great prophetic seed of the present passing into the future."[22] Young's reaction to the play, however, was completely negative, and he added that he hoped he did not give the impression that he was regarding the historical-personal import of *The Searching Wind* as a serious parable of our time. "This is a very poor transmuting of [our time] into dramatic art," he wrote.[23]

Nevertheless, Hellman posed a legitimate problem deserving analysis in the competitive relationship between Emily and Cassie. Like Zoe Akins, who had presented a similar relationship in *The Old Maid* the decade before, Hellman studied the behavior of two women over a twenty-year period, examining what effects society had on them and finding that their personal values, set against social unrest and turmoil, were dominated by the confusion of the identities as to which woman was really the heroine and which the villainess.

Emily takes advantage of Cassie's indecision about her marriage to Alex and marries him herself with no compunctions. Cassie adopts amoral reasoning when she begins her affair with Alex, and her confession at the end of the play reveals a baser motive which she has tried not to believe: her attraction to Alex was motivated by her anger and her desire to punish Emily. Her regret, which Hellman repeats in her view of world affairs, is that she has been unable to recognize these motives in herself. She admits that all three of them were frivolous people having no understanding of what they were doing and why they did it.[24]

It was Kappo Phelan's opinion, expressed in his review of the play in *Commonweal*, that Hellman had displayed her adult characters in an "uneasy, scattered morality" which she had not been willing to define.[25] But the confused morality which surrounds the two women is precisely the issue. The characters are placed purposely in times and places in which moral issues are undefinable and the ability to grasp the implications of certain actions (such as Alex's unfortunate decision to recommend appeasement and Cassie's determination to continue her alliance with Alex after his marriage to Emily) is obscured. But, as Hellman maintains, confusion results in both human and world affairs, although true moral values exist as constants no matter how human beings attempt to bend them to their advantage. Cassie discovers this after confessing her real reason for resuming her romance with Alex. Alex comes to the conclusion that sometimes he was wrong because he knew no better and sometimes he was wrong for reasons he could not explain.

Another success of the 1943-44 season was *Outrageous Fortune* by Rose Franken, a play which maintained interest in domestic drama but was centrally based in an anti-semitic theme, among other social problems. In contrast with the guileless Claudia, the central figure of this controversial drama is self-assured and worldly Crystal Grainger. One of the playwright's own favorites, *Outrageous Fortune* was considered the most morally debatable, yet the most intelligently written, of the early season plays.[26] It was received enthusiastically by some critics but aroused hostility in others for its bold exposition of a host of disputatious topics including anti-semitism, homosexuality, suicide, and marital frigidity. Burton

Rascoe, of the *New York World Telegram*, predicted divergent reactions to the play. Indeed, as Mantle recorded, for ten weeks after
its opening arguments for and against the play's statements and
conclusions were "freely spoken."[27]

A wealthy Jewish family comes together for a weekend at
their home in the country at which time a guest arrives, Crystal
Grainger. She is a woman of great dignity and magnetism, but is
suffering from a fatal heart condition. Attempting to restore peace
and self-respect to the troubled family members, she dies, but succeeds in giving the family a more tolerant perspective of themselves.

Crystal personifies the theme of the play through her tolerance, intelligence, understanding, and acceptance. Franken proposes
that aberrant behavior is common to all human beings and that to
accept and understand abnormalities is the only available solution,
albeit an uneasy one, to people of all races in comprehending the
turmoil of social and familial relationships. The theme was at once
the source of conflict among some critics who demanded a clearer
moral position from the playwright and the point of interest among
those who found that such a theme, although unsettled, was ultimately a more intelligent view of life than those offered by most of
the other plays of the season.[28]

Ironically, Crystal, the catalytic non-conformist, is the only
stable individual in a situation of misfits and maintains centrality
throughout the drama. She is seen as a traditional dying stage cour-
tesan by Wyatt. But Franken attempted to transcend the typical
traits of such a character by endowing her with greater breadth.
Initially she is distrusted by the family. Before her arrival she is
discussed as the most talked-of woman in America; Bert, the head of
the family, dismisses her as "riff raff." Yet it is from Crystal that
both Julian and Bert recognize their own lack of pride in their
Jewish heritage. As she confronts each character Crystal displays an
unpretentious ability to dissolve prejudices. Eventually, all are drawn
to her by her wisdom and tolerance, as well as her sexual attractiveness.

The enigma of her character is founded in what Mary Anne

Ferguson discusses as the "seductress-goddess" stereotype of woman. Her appeal is super-human, and, like Ferguson's model, Crystal "speaks through her tortured body paradoxical answers to existential questions."[29] Her "doctrine of purity," explained to Bert in characteristically oblique phrases, dismisses the existence of vice thus justifying her unrestrained mode of life.

Crystal's mystified male observers acknowledge her power by allowing her to influence them to want to do great and noble things. Barry, her musician companion who doubts his masculinity, explains that it takes a quality of greatness to be Crystal's lover, a quality which he feels he does not have. Yet Crystal is not a complete stereotype. Contrary to a classical concept of the seductress whose effect on men is often disastrous, Franken's heroine ennobles men while exonerating herself from guilt or censure because she maintains her own brand of integrity. And her function is not altogether biological. She is a seductress with a mind. George Jean Nathan recognized her as not merely a device for the manipulation of plot but as a character whose emotions are "filtered through her intellect."[30] To the family with false virtue she explains that Julian's homosexuality, Madeliene's unfulfilled desires, Bert's racial shame are the responsiblity of all of them and they must recognize that some of them *need* to sin in order to become sinless.[31] In this character Franken created an active representative of woman's fantasy, the woman who demands the freedom to choose her own way of life, who is endowed with great wisdom as well as admired for her overwhelming power of attraction.

Like *Outrageous Fortune, Pick Up Girl*, another successful drama of the 1943-44 season, stressed social ills and emphasized the misery that resulted from a problem which was increasingly apparent during war-time. Its author, Elsa Shelley, was a young actress married to a playwright, Irving Kaye Davis; she became interested in the subject of the effects of the war economy on the juveniles of poorer families in New York City. Shelley wrote *Pick Up Girl* as an accurately detailed court hearing of a female delinquent, and, in conjunction with the Michael Todd staff, it was presented May 3, 1944. Set in its entirety in a juvenile court, the stark realism of the drama was emphasized by the replication of the courtroom which Shelley had visited as a privileged guest while gathering her material.

Shelley was concerned with the alarming predicament of the overflow of juvenile delinquency cases which had been brought to the courts since the beginning of the war. In particular the increase of cases in New York City's Children's Courtroom appeared to be catastrophic. Mantle stated that inevitably the subject would reach the stage in the form of "fairly sordid realism" sooner or later, and Shelley's play demonstrated the need for explicating the problem.[32]

Public reaction to the play was surprisingly favorable in light of its explicit references to syphilis, pimping, abortion, and the clandestine organizations of youth gangs headed by adults whose purpose was to profit from the services of teen-aged boys and girls whom they lured into entertaining servicemen and wealthy business men. Mantle referred to the drama as a "social service" play which considered the case of endangered adolescents who had fallen victim to the "war fever," and their desire to do something to brighten the lives of servicemen.[33] Audiences, he said, were frankly curious about the subject and displayed their interest with steady attendance.

Critical reaction, however, was skeptical and several objections were offered. For example, the subject matter was considered timely but, as some critics felt, too sordid to be entertaining. Willella Waldorf of the *New York Evening Post* wrote:

> There is only one decent reason for writing and producing such a record as *Pick Up Girl* and we prefer to believe that its sponsors were moved by a genuine feeling that such a story told on a Broadway stage, as realistically as possible, might call attention to a festering sociological condition in need of far more drastic remedies than any of the well-meaning steps so far taken to combat it.[34]

Shelley herself was attacked for being naive in her social purpose. Wolcott Gibbs, *The New Yorker* drama critic, applauded her thesis but stated that as a playwright,

she is florid, conventional, and, I'm afraid, more than a little
innocent, with a tendency to approach prostitution with that
same enthusiastic and youthful bounce characteristic of a
"literary social worker" or a young and sentimental reporter
after his first assignment to night court.[35]

In addition, some reviewers doubted that the situation of war-time
delinquency was not being exploited for commercial reasons since
Shelley obviously had presented no solution to its curbing. But the
playwright, meeting the negative responses, answered those critics
by stating that exposure was her only aim and that it was her hope
that the story would direct attention to society's responsiblity. In
fact, her intention was indicated in the original title of the drama,
Elizabeth vs. You and Me.

Shelley's purpose was accomplished to some degree. Rosamond Gilder reported in her review of the play that a New York
magistrate, a woman, sent a young female delinquent to see the
production as an effective teaching method. Wyatt found that
Shelley's case was no isolated tragedy and was moved to uncover
startling statistics in her comments on the drama; assisting Shelley's
cause, she published the following information: 90 percent of the
youth who were being supervised in juvenile shelters in New York
City were under eighteen years of age and 50 percent were girls
under sixteen. *Pick Up Girl*, Wyatt concluded, was "a timely but
horrifying warning . . . for anyone with a social conscience."[36]

This was Shelley's first and only substantial success as a playwright, but it was not her initial intention to become a writer. Born
in Russia, she had come to the United States with her family and had
begun studying acting at an early age. Her first appearance had been
in a small part opposite Ethel Barrymore in *The Lady of the Camel-
ias*. Her most notable performance had been as Juliet to Walter
Hampden's Romeo, but illness had kept her from continuing her
acting career. In the meantime, she had married playwright Irving
Kaye Davis, and occupied herself by assisting her husband's playwriting efforts. It was during this time that she began collecting data
about the problems of young people and their difficulties in time of
war.

Shelley's protagonist, Elizabeth Collins, is a fifteen-year old girl brought to court on charges of performing immoral acts with a forty-seven-year old man. Her case history indicates that she is the eldest of four children for whom she is responsible while her mother works as a full-time cook in the evenings. Her father, unable to find work in New York, is working in a California shipyard, attempting to earn enough money to get the family out of debt. Elizabeth has become involved with a group of teenagers who entertain men for favors, clothing, jewelry, and money. She has had a brief affair with a young sailor who has since been shipped overseas. This has resulted in an illegal abortion performed on her by a physician friend of one of the group. Unknown to her and the older man who has seduced her, she has contracted syphilis from the sailor. After hearing the testimony of the witnesses who convince him that Elizabeth is redeemable, the judge sends her to Bellevue Hospital to be treated and· then to the State Training School for Girls for the next three years.

It was Shelley's intention to present Elizabeth's case as typical. This tended to reduce some of the other characters to stereotypes. The judge, for example, is presented as all-knowing and all-understanding; and Peter, Elizabeth's sixteen-year old violinist boyfriend, resorts to pathetic heroics in an effort to help Elizabeth escape and nobly stands by his promise of marriage in spite of her physical condition. But in the character of Elizabeth the playwright created an honest portrait of a confused young girl whose awareness of the implications of her situation is obscured by her desire to break away from overwhelming responsibilites at home. Shelley described her as a shy girl whose maturing figure belies her fifteen years and whose only model of success is the coarse and impudent sixteen-year old gang leader, Ruby. But in contrast to the one-dimensional Ruby, Elizabeth has compensatory characteristics which place her above the conventional pattern of the characters surrounding her. Shelley perceives in Elizabeth a complex pattern of human behavior in the girl's contradictory impulses to love her family, yet at the same time revolt against it. Elizabeth displays compassion for her mother even though she has been neglected by her; she realizes that her mother has been poorly educated, has few skills by which to earn adequate wages, and has had to assume most of the responsibility for raising four children during the depression and war. The contradiction materializes when Mrs. Collins accuses Elizabeth of being promiscuous and the hysterical girl calls her a liar and strikes her. But immediately she begs her forgiveness and seeks consolation from her. Yet the fact of her mother's needs is the precise cause of Elizabeth's revolt. At the same time she seeks her mother's protection, she attempts to shake off her mother's image. Her most prized possession is a fur-trimmed jacket given to her by a man at one of Ruby's parties which she regards as a symbol of the sources which will fill her own needs.

In spite of the dated street-idiom dialogue, Elizabeth's youthful joy of life, which, in her social surroundings, is at the same time the source of her bewilderment, is expressed in a poignant moment when she is alone with Peter. She tells him that she is unable to understand her feelings of wanting to love and be loved and for that reason she feels she must be a bad girl.

Shelley also pointed to the limitations of the court in its capacity to deal with Elizabeth's personal need to define herself and find self worth. The judge realizes that her delinquency is the outgrowth of intricate moral causes which are too complicated for the law to handle. Therefore, his judgment is based on the expedient that her case is typical of hundreds of other juvenile delinquents who must be dealt with promptly, even if the causes and cure have not yet been found. It was this impersonal disposal of Elizabeth's plight that caused the critics to be dissatisfied with Shelley's conclusion, but Shelley, being faithful to the reality of the situation, could do no more than indicate Elizabeth's bleak future.

The end of the 1944-45 season marked the beginning of new trends in American drama. The theatre began recovering slowly from its post-war hangover, producing unsteady seasons, the majority of plays being revivals of the classics. But between 1946 and 1948 a new creative enthusiasm was noted by Hewes in those playwrights who were relieved of the war-time need for relevance. Returning to more aesthetic experimentation, a new and better kind of theatre was sought by some dramatists, although, according to Hewes, "no one knew what this should be"; and "experimental' and 'repertory' were tossed around with innocent reverence."[37]

For women writers it was a time for resuming their concerns with women-centered material. Lillian Hellman in 1946 presented a protracted analysis of Regina Hubbard and the rest of the Hubbard family whom she originated in *The Little Foxes* in 1939, calling this work *Another Part of the Forest*. The play arrested the attention of both audiences and critics, not so much for its achievement as an integration of her earlier success, as for the shock value of the characters who were even more intensely avaricious and grasping than their earlier embodiments.

Interestingly, Hellman's reasons for returning to the family for further dramatic examination were based upon reactions she had felt from those who saw *The Little Foxes* and were morally offended by the actions of the family. To Lucius Beebe, journalist for the *New York Herald Tribune*, Hellman explained her motivation for writing the play:

> You can imagine that after living with *The Little Foxes* for several years, I got to be on pretty chatty terms with the Hubbard family . . . I knew them inside out, and while no more tolerant of their rapacity and avarice, I began to feel a mixture of sentiments toward them which in no way derived from anything they themselves represented. I began to dislike the audience hypocrisy by the terms of which people who saw the show seemed to derive a feeling of moral superiority to the Hubbards. . . . This gave me a sort of jolt. It did not change my graveyard affection for the Hubbards, whom I cherish as one would cherish a nest of particularly vicious diamond-back rattlesnakes, but it did make me feel that it was worthwhile to look into their family background and find out what it was that made them the nasty people they were.[38]

From this it can be assumed that Hellman was interested primarily in the psychological causes for family evil rather than in social commentary as she had been in *The Little Foxes*. John Mason Brown in the *Saturday Review* suggested that what her first play managed to say about an exploiting Southern class as personified in the Hubbards, *Another Part of the Forest* said about them only as a "peculiar and horrendous family."[39] From father to son, the evil is relinquished as if it were a birthright, particularizing Hellman's theme that not only are the sins of the father passed on to the sons, but the capacity for sinning as well.

Brown found that psychologically the play piled "horror . . . upon horror," out of the "wholesale villainy" of the characters.[40] It was agreed that Hellman's characters surpassed those of *The Little Foxes* in their vicious treatment of one another, and, as Krutch observed in *The Nation*, that by comparison the first play "would have to be ranked as an idyl."[41]

The action of the play takes place in 1880 at the Alabama mansion of Marcus Hubbard, the despotic and despised store owner who has made his fortune during the Civil War as a traitor to the South and who escaped being lynched years before for having caused a massacre of a regiment of Southern soldiers, some of them his own neighbors and friends. Lavinia, his deranged wife, yearns to cleanse herself of the sins of her loveless marriage by leaving Marcus and devoting the rest of her life to the teaching of black children. She and her black servant are the only ones who know of Marcus' past treachery and have secretly written an account of his actions the night of the massacre, providing proof of his guilt. By double-cross and persuasion, Ben, the older, importunate son who has been ruled by his father's tyranny, learns of the secret testimony and is able to manipulate his father's downfall. He assumes all of his father's wealth and interests and is thereby able to dictate the futures of the twenty-year old Regina, who loses her lover and will be forced to marry the wealthy and genteel Horace Giddens, and of Oscar, whose "deep and sincere" romance with the town prostitute, is shattered when Ben arranges to have him marry Birdie Bagtry.

In characterization, Hellman's focus is centered on the relationship of the father and his eldest son; their power struggle as it shifts advantage from one to the other, creates a compelling, if not appalling, situation. But the interest of this study is with Regina, and *Another Part of the Forest* offers an illuminating view of this character in her youth.

Regina's capacity to struggle for family power is immature in this work; her actions are governed first by her father, then by Ben,

as her ability to act on her own is suppressed. Nevertheless, she is
depicted as the only member of the family who can influence Marcus
and has already learned tricks of persuasion and placation which have
earned her the position of being her father's favorite. Her character
already points to an extreme ruthlessness in getting her own way in
things, as well as a highly developed sense of knowing her limitations
as the only female in a family of male cut-throats and opportunists.
Her mother, who has been victimized by her husband's violent will,
has sought refuge in religion and eccentricity and is a despicable
model to Regina. Like her brother Ben, Regina is dominated by the
passions of her father, and her vicious nature is an inevitable exten-
sion of his. Under such circumstances Regina has only two alternatives for behavior: weak submission as found in both Lavinia,
whose choice has led her to insanity, and in Birdie, who, in *The
Little Foxes*, become a reflection of Lavinia; or adoption of the
mode of behavior which has sustained the male members of the family and has placed them in positions of power. There is no doubt as
to which alternative is the more attractive to Regina. She is already
well on her way to becoming the evil character of Hellman's earlier
play.

By contrast, Fay Kanin wrote the nostalgic drama, *Goodbye,
My Fancy*, in 1948 in an attempt to articulate a woman's need for
returning to her past. In the process she presented a view of the post-
war version of the "new woman" who represented current feminine
ideals. Kanin's main character, Agatha Reed, epitomized the post-
war image of the educated career woman who had forgone marriage
and children during the war and was now ready to complete her
busy life with the acquisitions of home and husband.

Actress, radio and movie writer, Fay Kanin wrote *Goodbye,
My Fancy* after a visit to her alma mater, Elmira College. Remin-
iscences of her undergraduate days gave her the material for her
first full-length play. Kanin had worked in Hollywood at RKO
studios, writing film scenarios and network radio programs. During
the war she wrote and narrated a radio program called *The Woman's
Angle*, by which she expressed feminist theories which, as Burns
Mantle described them, took the point of view that "women were
just as good as men."[42] She married Michael Kanin, screenwriter

and brother of playwright-director Garson Kanin; her husband produced *Goodbye, My Fancy* in November, 1947.

The play received a good-humored response from the critics
who generally felt that Kanin had achieved an intelligent, adult
approach to several important questions of a post-war society even
though the form of the play was considered comic by some. Brooks
Atkinson of the *New York Times* referred to it as the type of comedy that had developed in the past years; like "painless dentistry,"
he said, "it is good for you and does not hurt."[43]

The theme of the play is Kanin's curiosity about times past,
specifically, what happens to individuals when they attempt to
recapture the past. In this retrospection Kanin concluded that the
past cannot be revived and lived as the present. Kanin's protagonist,
Agatha, in recalling why she accepted candidacy for congress and
why she has devoted most of her life to public service, states the
theme: no one can afford the luxury of status quo, and not to go
forward means to go back.[44]

Interwoven with the playwright's intention to present this
central idea were several forthright opinions regarding the values of
education, moral integrity, women's rights, and the importance of
realistic goals. These subjects were all used as background for the
situations that confront the main character, Agatha, the liberal
congresswoman and former war correspondent who returns to her
old college to receive an honorary degree, an irony to Agatha since
she was expelled from college in her junior year for staying out all
night with a man. These circumstances have remained secret, however, mainly because the man in question, James Merrill, to whom
Agatha was engaged, is now the president of the college. Agatha
attempts to recapture her past romance by resuming her relationship with the now-widowed Jim, but finds that complications ensue
when she insists on the right to show a documentary film against
war which she has written and narrated herself and has brought with
her to acquaint the young graduates with the horrors of war. But the
trustees of the school force the president to acquiese to their refusal
to allow its presentation. Agatha, disenchanted with Merrill's passivity and subjugation to the businessmen who finance the college,

realizes that both of them have changed; since she is unwilling to compromise her ideals, she finds that her real love is with the straightforward *Life* magazine photographer, Matt Cole, who is there covering her homecoming and who has been pursuing her for the past six years.

In spite of some negative comments from critics who felt that Kanin's philosophy was specious, the playwright apparently succeeded in presenting a portrait of the "new woman" of the 1940s whose combined intelligence and glamor allowed her to play a non-conventional role. Indeed, as Kanin presented her, Agatha is the representation of an ideal to millions of American women, the active, important woman they think they'd like to be. One of the female students, anticipating her arrival, surmises that Agatha will probably be unattractive, wear sturdy low-heeled shoes, and dress in tailored tweeds. Instead, of course, Agatha is tall, blond, slender, and smartly dressed, and is remembered as being one of the best war correspondents to report during the war by all who worked with her.

In addition to her physical attractiveness, she is a shrewd politician who has benefited from her wartime experiences as a correspondent. This is evidenced by another ideal which she embodies: the incorruptibility of common sense. As a congresswoman she is devoted to the work of exposing the realities of war and educating the public to the terror of another war which would undoubtedly be more destructive than the last one. But her attempt to show her film, which is frank, anti-war propaganda, is met with male resistance, prejudice, and complacency by the board of trustees. Her confrontation with Griswold, a wealthy business man and member of the board, is the device used by Kanin to expose Agatha's integrity and the idealism she represents. Griswold, who has profited from the war and is now chief dictator of policy for the college, explains his objections to Agatha's film by placating her. Agatha, understanding his sidestepping referral to her "specialness" as a tough woman, turns the discussion back to the real issue of her purpose in showing the film and challenges the board to let the students judge her presentation for themselves. But Griswold believes there is too much "scaremongering" going on and feels that wars will not stop simply because the younger generation is forced to face its horrors. The children, he says, should be able to have fun while they are young without having to face the possibilities of another war until they are forced to. To this proposition Agatha responds that it is in the hands and power of the young to stop another war from happening if they know what war means, that is, if they are actually allowed to see its effects.

Kanin's concept of the post-war female ideal is an interesting variation on the theme of the successful and feminine liberated woman. Kanin also points to a weakness in the image. Although Agatha is financially independent, self-sufficient, intelligent, as well as physically attractive, her life style has one important deficiency: she lacks a home and husband. Her privileged status has given her a busy life, to be sure, but what she really wants is a full life, which means a marriage that would not demand the sacrificing of her acquired freedoms. Her peculiar and unlikely attraction to Matt Cole completes Kanin's portrait of the "new woman" of the post-war era.

Carson McCullers adapted her novel, *The Member of the Wedding*, for the stage in 1940. The intimacy required to stage her play and its loose structure reinforced the realization that the old proscenium stage and strict well-made play form of the past were in conflict with the needs of playwrights who sought subconscious levels of characterization and required audiences to be closer to onstage events.

In contrast to Kanin's sophisticated "liberated" woman of the 1940s who possessed fame, high political status, leadership, and was considered a paragon of womanly ideals, McCullers emphasized the simple image of a child making awkward attempts to attain such status.

McCullers had had very little experience with the theatre before this first play was produced. In fact, Mantle pointed out, before her success as a playwright she had seen only six plays, four of them school plays and two Broadway shows, and her only previous instruction in playwriting had been the advice to "go ahead and write."[45]

As a novelist, McCullers was ranked high on the list of contemporary American writers before *The Member of the Wedding* was adapted for the stage. She had come to New York City to study as a concert pianist and had taken varied jobs to support herself at Columbia University and New York University. Soon her preoccupation with short story writing led her to two Guggenheim fellowships and an award from the American Academy of Arts and Letters.

Mantle viewed McCullers as "surrounded by an aura of genius and success" even before her career as a playwright began.[46] After the success of the stage version of *The Member of the Wedding*, she continued to write, although her work was not strictly confined to the theatre. Her better-known theatre efforts were *The Square Root of Wonderful* in 1958, and her story, *The Ballad of the Sad Cafe*, which was adapted to the stage by Edward Albee in 1963.

The Member of the Wedding, presented in January, 1950, was the first "hit" of the year and won the Drama Critics Circle Award as the best play of the 1949-50 season. But its producers at first were not confident that it would be successful since its tryout had brought the general reaction that it would be too weak to compete with New York commercialism. The general consensus was that the production would get good notices but would die after one week. Yet the play achieved artistic and financial success, running 174 performances in 1950 and continued to run to the end of that season.

There was a quality about the play which eluded the critics. Charmed by McCullers' delicate perception of character, nevertheless the critics were unprepared for the liberties the playwright took with dramatic conventions. In their view the play did not seem to have the polish and form of the ideally constructed drama. As a novelist, McCullers was highly praised for her tendency to follow her main character's stream of consciousness rather than shape it into a more coherent form; but, when she transferred the same technique to the stage, some critics objected to what they saw as a formless and non-climactic style which, they felt, could only be regarded as a weakness in her playwriting. Wolcott Gibbs of *The New Yorker* magazine commented that although he felt that *The Member of the*

Wedding was the first serious new play of any consequence that season, it was not entirely satisfactory from a theatrical point of view; he stated that the principal trouble was that McCullers had tried to be too literal in her transference of the book to the stage which resulted in a "curiously uneven work."[47] And theatre reviewer Kappo Phelan was ambiguous in his reaction, calling the plåy "a complete delight," yet feeling dissatisfied with the way in which McCullers presented the theme of a child's solution to identity.[48]

But to others she appeared as a leader of a new form of drama whose loose and non-conclusive structure was more representative of contemporary thought than the tight-knit construction of the past. McCullers presented her point of view in the April, 1950, issue of *Theatre Arts Magazine*, in which she stated that she could not comment on the critical controversy which surrounded her non-conforming work because its design was intuitive, and she, approaching it subjectively as the artist, could only "precipitate the inherent reactions."[49] Furthermore, her drama was unconventional, she explained, because it was not meant as a literal work, but as an "inward" play, just as the conflicts and its values were meant to be abstract. For example, the antagonist was intended to be the human condition of life, the sense of moral isolation; and the play itself was to be concerned with the "weight of time, the hazard of human existence, bolts of chance."[50] The aesthetic concept, she explained, was misunderstood by some who could not see that the reaction of the characters to the abstract phenomena actually forwarded the movement of the play.

In theme *The Member of the Wedding* presents the view that loneliness is a particular torture of youth in the process of developing a consciousness of self. The adolescent Frankie is desperate to belong to someone; this is dramatized in her insistence that she go along with her brother and new sister-in-law on their honeymoon. She has come to believe that they are the "we" of herself. Frankie's youthful searching is balanced by the character of Berenice, the black housekeeper, who knows that loneliness in life is inevitable. She is able to bear her own personal grief with understanding even when faced with the loss of her foster brother, seven-year old John Henry, and, finally, Frankie herself.

The simple plot reveals twelve-year old Frankie living in Georgia with her widowed father and Berenice, her surrogate mother, as she prepares for her brother's wedding. Out of a desire to belong and her adolescent adoration for the couple, she fantasizes a new, exciting life with the newly-weds; but when her plan to accompany them on the honeymoon is thwarted, she runs away. She returns to find her seven-year old cousin, John Henry, who was her constant companion and only playmate, dying of meningitis. Months pass, John Henry has died, and Frankie and her father are moving away, leaving Berenice behind.

Frankie is a collection of curious traits which make her character seem slightly incoherent and somewhat "immune to the usual rules of human behavior."[51] But her behavior seems to be a composite portrait of the sometimes baffling, sometimes transparent actions of the human young which often defy the usual rules. Rosalind Miles, describing Frankie's fears as being the source of her erratic temperament, suggested that the aimlessness and incoherence in her life were recognizable as commonplace adolescent behavior and the development of a consciousness.[52] The transition from childhood to youth, which is McCullers' theme, is the background for the direction-testing of Frankie's new awareness of herself.

Her personality is extravagant yet authentic mainly because of the playwright's emphasis on the inward conflicts in Frankie's life. As McCullers wrote, her twelve-year old portrays a sense of moral isolation, but the portrait is complicated, as it is in life, by what McCullers saw as a "lyric tragi-comic" element in human nature which she felt had to be included in Frankie's makeup.[53] Indeed, McCullers worried that perhaps the co-existence of Frankie's funniness and grief would confuse an audience, but, in drawing a fine line between Frankie's two extreme characteristics, McCullers actually was indicating her own artistic perceptions of the elusive nature of the human soul. In her description McCullers emphasized Frankie's seemingly antithetic qualities: she is a gangling girl, yet dreamy and restless; her periods of unfocused energy alternate with rapt concentration upon her inner world of fantasy.[54] After the engaged couple leaves, Frankie disconsolately wanders about the house, puzzled by her inner feelings, experiencing overwhelming loneliness. Her plaintive plea for recognition is immediately followed by a wish for some cold peach ice cream. Thus as Frankie experiences the confusion of her emotions, she attempts to define herself by a predictably illogical rationale. She becomes breathlessly amazed by life and this instant introspection leads to the conclusion that she must accompany her brother on his wedding trip in order to find the "we" person of herself to take the place of the lonely "I." After a wild display of excitement over how her life will change, she is calmed in a tender moment by the stolid and sensitive Berenice. Exhausted, Frankie suddenly becomes aware of her own mortality and realizes too that the world itself is quick and finite. She realizes this again, months later, when she and Berenice talk about the changes that have taken place in their lives and how their paths are separating. For Frankie "fate" has brought her new friends and a new world in which to live; for Berenice it is a sad moment when she realizes that Frankie's new world is already strange to her. In the closing moments of the play McCullers presents a parallel study of loneliness in the rebellious alienation of the child which finds a cure, and the patient isolation of the woman which does not.

By 1950 the theatre, having survived a post-depression period, the effects of world war, and post-war readjustments, had become "much more neurotic" than it had been at the beginning of the decade; and the pressures placed upon producers, playwrights, directors, and actors for "smash hits" had a stifling effect on most new playwrights.[55] At this point dramatists began turning to the off-Broadway stages in an effort to showcase their new works. The strength of the off-Broadway movement began to be felt, to be regarded later as an important outlet for women playwrights of the 1960s.

Notes

[1]Henry Hewes, ed., *Famous American Plays of the 1940's* (New York: Dell Publishing Co., Inc., 1967), p. 11.

[2]Burns Mantle, *The Best Plays of 1940-41* (New York: Dodd, Mead and Company, 1941), p. 64.

[3]John Gassner, "Lillian Hellman," in *The Oxford Companion to the Theatre*, ed. by Phyllis Hartnoll (London: Oxford University, 1972), p. 438.

[4]Rosamond Gilder, "Prizes that Bloom in the Spring," in *Theatre Arts Monthly*, 25, No. 6 (June 1941), p. 409.

[5]Euphemia Van Rensselaer Wyatt, "The Drama: 'Watch on the Rhine,' " in *The Catholic World*, 153 (May 1941), p. 409.

[6]Louis Kronenberger, "PM Review," in *Watch on the Rhine* by Lillian Hellman (New York: Random House, 1941), p. 172.

[7]Lillian Hellman, *Watch on the Rhine* (New York: Random House, 1941), I. p. 48.

[8]*Idem.*

[9]Kronenberger, "PM Review," p. 172.

[10]*Idem.*

[11]Lillian Hellman, *Pentimento: A Book of Portraits* (Boston: Little, Brown and Company, 1973), p. 184.

[12]Mantle, *Ibid.*, p. 360.

[13]Rosamond Gilder, "When the Earth Quakes," in *Theatre Arts Monthly*, 25, No. 4 (April 1941), p. 263.

13a"New Plays in Manhattan," in *Time* Magazine, 37, No. 8 (24 February 1941), p. 58.

14Rose Franken, *Claudia* (New York: Farrar & Rinehart, Inc., 1941), III, p. 189.

15Burns Mantle, *The Best Plays of 1941-42* (New York: Dodd, Mead and Company, 1942), p. 2.

16*Ibid.*, p. 7.

17*Idem.*

18*Ibid.*, pp. 349-350.

19Burns Mantle, *The Best Plays of 1943-44* (New York: Dodd, Mead and Company, 1944), p. 69.

20*Ibid.*, p. 70.

21*Ibid.*, p. 69.

22Stark Young, "Behind the Beyond," in *The New Republic*, 110, No. 18 (1 May 1944), p. 604.

23*Idem.*

24Lillian Hellman, *The Searching Wind* (New York: The Viking Press, 1944), III, iii, p. 90.

25Kappo Phelan, "The Stage and Screen," in *Commonweal*, 40, No. 2 (28 April 1944), p. 40.

26Mantle, *The Best Plays of 1943-44*, p. 8.

27*Idem.*

28*Idem.*

29Mary Anne Ferguson, *Images of Women in Literature* (Palo Alto: Houghton Mifflin, 1973), p. 171.

[30] George Jean Nathan, *The Theatre Book of the Year, 1943-44* (New York: Alfred A. Knopf, 1945), p. 116.

[31] Rose Franken, *Outrageous Fortune* (Los Angeles: Samuel French, 1944), II, p. 102.

[32] Mantle, *The Best Plays of 1943-44*, p. 315.

[33] *Ibid.*, p. 15.

[34] *Ibid.*, p. 315.

[35] Wolcott Gibbs, "A Pamphlet Comes to Town," in *The New Yorker*, 20, No. 13 (13 May 1944), p. 265.

[36] Euphemia Van Rensselaer Wyatt, "The Drama," in *The Catholic World*, 159 (June 1944), p. 265.

[37] Hewes, *Famous American Plays of the 1940's*, p. 16.

[38] Burns Mantle, *The Best Plays of 1946-47* (New York: Dodd, Mead and Company, 1947), p. 163.

[39] John Mason Brown, "Seeing Things," in *The Saturday Review of Literature*, 29, No. 51 (21 December 1946), p. 20.

[40] *Idem.*

[41] Joseph Wood Krutch, "Drama," in *The Nation*, 163, No. 23 (7 December 1946), p. 670.

[42] Burns Mantle, *The Best Plays of 1947-48* (New York: Dodd, Mead and Company, 1948), p. 374.

[43] Fay Kanin, *Goodbye, My Fancy*, with a foreword by Brooks Atkinson (New York: Samuel French, 1947), p. 129.

[44] *Ibid.*, II, p. 48.

[45] Burns Mantle, *The Best Plays of 1949-50* (New York: Dodd, Mead and Company, 1950), p. 347.

[46]*Idem.*

[47]Wolcott Gibbs, "The Theatre," in *The New Yorker*, 25, No. 47 (14 January 1950), p. 46.

[48]Kappo Phelan, "The Stage," in *Commonweal*, 51, No. 16 (27 January 1950), p. 437.

[49]Carson McCullers, "The Vision Shared," in *Theatre Arts*, 34, No. 4 (April 1950), p. 30.

[50]*Idem.*

[51]Gibbs, "The Theatre," in *The New Yorker*, p. 46.

[52]Rosalind Miles, *The Fiction of Sex* (London: Vision Press, 1974), p. 142.

[53]McCullers, "The Vision Shared," p. 30.

[54]Carson McCullers, "The Member of the Wedding," in *Famous American Plays of the 1940's*, ed. by Henry Hewes (New York: Dell Publishing Co. Inc., 1967), I, pp. 373-74.

[55]Hewes, *Famous American Plays of the 1940's*, p. 21.

Chapter IV

1950-1960

The theatre of the 1950s was part of a society beset with the problems of inflationary economics, cold war, and personal frustration. In demonstrating these social fluxes the theatre itself was a paradox which, according to Lee Strasberg, director of the Actor's Studio in New York and editor of the *Famous American Play* series for the decade, at once seemed to inspire the feeling of having "hit bottom," evidenced by numerous and disappointing plays, while at the same time it produced O'Neill's *Long Day's Journey Into Night*, "the greatest American play of our time."[1] There were many important playwrights but fewer important plays being written. This was particularly true of women playwrights who, after establishing themselves as serious dramatists during the decades of the forties and thirties, seemed inexplicably silent except for an increase in their output as comedy writers.

From this ten-year period only four plays are considered, all of which were substantial works which elicited serious comment from critics. The plays were Lillian Hellman's 1950 drama, *The Autumn Garden* and her 1960 work, *Toys in the Attic*; Jane Bowles' first and only play, *In the Summer House* (1953); and Lorraine Hansberry's *A Raisin in the Sun* (1959). Two of the four, *A Raisin in the Sun* and *Toys in the Attic*, won the Drama Critics Circle Award.

The 1950-51 season was described by *Best Plays* editor John Chapman as one lacking new playwrights. Keeping the stage alive were the veterans of the past decade, Arthur Miller and Tennessee Williams, but no new playwrights seemed to be writing. The preponderant dramatic form, moreover, was adaptation rather than original works. Chapman proposed that commercial value, more highly regarded by backers and producers than artistic achievement, was a discouraging factor confronting new writers. Even established playwrights attempted to secure recognition by working with ready-made material. Lillian Hellman experimented with the musical *Candide*, but her past original works had met with more estimable criticism. Yet, in 1950 she wrote one of her most powerful character studies, *The Autumn Garden*. Chapman felt this to be her best play in its examination of the irresolute lives of a group of middle-aged individuals.

With this work, Hellman attempted a different approach to her dramatic material. *The Autumn Garden* displayed her desire to break with the tight-knit formula with which she had achieved prominence in the past by emphasizing both the sad and funny frailties of human beings and by experimenting with a style characteristic of the Russian playwright, Anton Chekhov.

Critical reaction to Hellman's experimentaiton was ambivalent compared to past criticism of her work. John Lardner, critic for *The New Yorker*, felt that audiences, used to her former direct, uncompromising style, might be disappointed in the play. Hellman, he claimed, was best known for plays that "hit the audience between the eyes with one clean, crisp punch."[2] Indeed, the most notable things about Hellman's previous works were that they were well planned, were admirably constructed, and were distinguished by the force of her moral anger; but Lardner projected that admirers of *The Children's Hour*, *The Little Foxes* and *Watch on the Rhine* might miss Hellman's earlier, crusading mood when they saw *The Autumn Garden*.[3] Setting aside the questions raised by her stylistic changes, Lardner endorsed Hellman's talent, stating that the most important thing was that she was writing "without the cold fury of former times" and that she continued to show intelligence and craftsmanship in her current work.[4]

The universal daydream theme found in *The Autumn Garden* is presented in characters who believe that the setbacks and compromises of ordinary living will be somehow resolved, and that once present frustrations can be eliminated, they will experience serenity and happiness; but their dreams are revealed as delusions preventing them from living in the present. By presenting this notion as the expression of each of the characters, Hellman indicates their failure to recognize the present moment as the absolute condition of life. She presents this self-deception as the source which drains her characters of energy and mental stability, and their dilemma is complicated by the fact that in spite of their middle age, their daydreams still persist.

Hellman's previous technique of integrating plot with character is maintained in *The Autumn Garden*. An assorted group of people are gathered together as a yearly summer ritual in the summer house of Constance Tuckerman. Constance has been forced to make her living by renting the house every summer to her close friends and relatives. Added to the group this year are Nicholas Denery and his wife, Nina. Nick was an old beau of Constance's and, since his departure several years ago, has achieved dubious notoriety as a socialite painter. Upon his arrival the relationships of the characters are exposed, and each individual is revealed to be frustrated and unhappy in one way or another: Constance foolishly has anticipated a romantic reunion with Nick after his twenty-year absence, and has ignored her friend, Crossman, who at one time wanted to marry her; Nina recognizes that her life with Nick has been one of self-deception; and, at Nick's off-hand suggestion, Rose Griggs manages to tighten her hold on her unhappy husband. All harbor the illusion that someday their lives will be happy, but through a series of confrontations they each realize that they are incapable of changing their futures because gradually they have become the sum of their past lives. Only one character, Sophie, a war refugee who has been brought to the United States by Constance to work as her maid, is capable of facing her life realistically. She is able to avoid an indifferent marriage to the young, brow-beaten son of one of the summer guests and manages to extort enough money from Nina to return to her native country to choose her own way of life.

Hellman presented an unsentimental view of her characters as she revealed them caught up in the malaise of their daydreams. Walter Kerr commented that she drew together this group of people "rather arbitrarily," forcing each of them to confront the futile and devitalizing myth of a personal millenium.[5] Because she forced herself to remain objective towards her characters, Hellman imposed on them the painful recognition that their lives of compromise and substitutions were their ultimate reality and the full lives for which they had been waiting were the dream. The play ends, as Kerr concludes, in a kind of "Chekhovian stalemate," because when wished-for opportunities come, such as Constance's tardy realization of Crossman's love for her which has now dissipated into indifference, the characters are neither able nor willing to accept them.[6]

Hellman handled this diffused plot in multiple situations and parallel construction in which all the relationships come to similar results: emotional paralysis. This is particularly evident in the three major women characters. Rose Griggs uses her flirtatious, fun-loving image to hide her awareness of her husband's restless desire to be free from their marriage. Approaching middle-age and losing her once youthful feminine graces, she plays the fool when faced with the reality of her loveless marriage. Refusing to understand her husband's unhappiness, she rationalizes, then dismisses the real issues and attempts a ludicrous flirtation which reinforces Griggs' desire to leave her. When she is told that she has serious health problems, she begins to realize how trivial her life has been, but her established pattern of behavior will not allow her to seek inner strength or courage. As usual, she pleads for help from Griggs. Regretfully, Griggs agrees to stay with her until her health improves, knowing that Rose will never change, that her promise to give him a divorce after that time means nothing, and that he will live to like her even less than he does now.

In the same manner, Nina Denery, the chic but world-weary wife of the incorrigible painter, Nick, hides behind the image of the all-suffering, all-understanding, and forgiving wife. But her true motivation is based in her own self-contempt. As Nick points out to her, she seeks to demean herself and so chose to love him. Sophie also perceives this in her. By rejecting her charitable offer to send her back to her homeland, Sophie refuses to become the object of Nina's false benevolence. Instead, she demands that the money be considered as blackmail in compensation for Nick's irresponsible advances toward her. In this way Sophie will not have to be grateful to her. From these revelations of herself, Nina comes to the devastating realization that like Rose, she can never change; having made these compensations, she is now dependent upon them.

Likewise, the compensations made in Constance's life have resulted in a wasted existence in which she has carried on her prolonged infatuation with the unobtainable Nick. Having spent over twenty years waiting for him to return and staunchly clinging to the gentility of her well-born Southern background, she has become fussy and prim. Crossman, who has long since given up any hopes of marrying her, wryly describes her as the typical Southern lady who must sacrifice her life for something, anything.

Constance is appalled by Sophie's practical attitude toward her pre-arranged marriage to the son of a fanatically possessive woman. Her romantic ideals, which she herself has never acted upon, are offended because neither Sophie nor her fiance thinks love in their marriage is of great importance. Listening to Constance's views of what a perfect marriage should be, Crossman points out the sad, but funny irony of her life: her wisdom comes, he supposes, from not thinking. When Nick paints her portrait, deliberately emphasizing her aging and shabby appearance, Constance begins to realize the vanity of her fantasies. In a final desperate attempt to salvage her dream of being loved and taken care of by a good man, ironically she turns to Crossman, the now aimless, alcoholic bachelor. But he has learned to live with his unrequited love through the compensations of drink and is now powerless to accept her. When he refuses her offer of marriage the irony of her life is complete. Like Crossman, she accepts two sad but truthful conclusions that we lie to ourselves and that we choose to.[7]

These three women suffer from the same futile illusions about themselves and are equally devitalized by their dreams of a fuller life. They cannot avail themselves of reality because they have depended too much on the unattainable past to accept the possible present.

By the 1953-54 season Louis Kronenberger, the new editor

for the *Best Plays* series, noted that new playwrights were beginning to emerge and the season was more frutiful for their dramas. One of these new playwrights was Jane Bowles. Her stangely mixed comic-drama produced in 1953, *In the Summer House*, emphasized the vagaries of a dominant mother-submissive daughter relationship and explored the effects of destructive family love.

Bowles was recognized by Wyatt in *The Catholic World*, as a writer "with full presage of a great gift."[8] *In the Summer House* was Bowles' first play and was derived from her story, *Two Serious Ladies*, which appeared in *Harper's Magazine* in the early 1940s. A self-taught linguist and world traveler, Bowles had established a high reputation for a small body of work as a writer of fiction and short stories before her brief career as a dramatist was launched. Her husband, composer Paul Bowles, wrote the incidental music for her drama.

Her play went through several revisions and tryouts before it reached the Playhouse Theatre in New York City on December 29, 1953. It received mixed notices, but in general critics agreed that its author was a fresh, original talent. Kronenberger stated that although the play "never truly turned into a *real* play," at its best it boasted of "the most individual and expressive writing of the season."[9] Although Wolcott Gibbs, *The New Yorker* critic, saw it as a queer, obscure piece, sometimes "over-burdened with labored and pretentious imagery," he concluded that its eloquence and path-os pointed to a basic integrity of purpose and he found the plot to be unusually intuitive, intelligent and compassionate.[10] The play's merits, he decided, outweighed its faults, and he rated it as an impressive serious play.

For Eric Bentley and many other critics, *In the Summer House* brought attention to the fact that the "new drama," which critics had come to associate with the works of Tennessee Williams, was a strong influence in the writing style of several of the younger and newer playwrights of the decade. Williams' apparent stress of atmosphere in lieu of plot, a pattern often disliked by more tra-ditionalist critics, was repeated in Bowles' play. *Commonweal* critic Richard Hayes indicated that the effects sought by Bowles were indeed derivative of the themes and techniques of the "new fiction"; as evidence of this he cited her "claustral focus" centered in her women characters and the attention paid to symbolic detail.[11] He related her work to her contemporary, Carson McCullers. The characters in the Bowles' drama, he stated,

> ... move in that ambience of emotional isolation recorded by Carson McCullers, among others, so movingly ... Mrs. Bowles has fashioned a work of intricate and seductive beauty, harmonious and subtle in its impact on the sensibility as a musical composition. And like a piece of music, it is accessible to criticism largely in terms of its modulation and coloring, its sensuous texture and expressive content.[12]

Some deficiencies were found in the "new drama," however. It was Eric Bentley's judgment that the "new" dramatist was not interested in events and morals, but in mood and psychology, "that is ... in melancholy and neurosis."[13] He also pointed out that the "new drama" expected to be an exception to the notion that a play was a condensed literary form; it was his contention that although it did have a form of sorts, the "new fiction" was not really suitable for drama. Specifically, Brooks Atkinson questioned the Williams-inspired style of *In the Summer House*. Was it enough, he asked, to be insightful about only one aspect of the lives of a small group of insignificant people? In defense of the new form, *Theatre Arts Magazine* took a positive view in its assessment of *In the Summer House*, stating that since Bowles' characters were real people, their dilemmas did matter, even if they were never resolved "in a manner that can be called conclusive or high voltage."[14]

Bowles' plot is a mixture of events, character studies, and moods. Set at the home of Gertrude Eastman-Cuevas on the coast of Southern California, the environment suggests the disorder of Mrs. Eastman-Cuevas' life. The house is run-down and the garden is in a disarray of dead vegetation. Nothing will grow except for the heavy vines that cover the small summer house where Molly, Gertrude's eighteen-year old daughter, spends most of her time dreaming and reading comics. Gertrude, a dominating and selfish woman, has had a childhood of jealous attachment to her father who did not return her affection. After his death she had married a Spaniard who never met her high expectations based on the ideals she held of her father. When her husband died, she was forced to take in boarders at the once stylish Spanish mansion which she and her daughter now inhabit. Molly is totally dominated by her mother whose treatment of her reflects her mother's obsession to recapture the essence of her own father's power. Molly is both fascinated by her mother's strength and overwhelmed by it, thus seeks refuge in the summer house as a way of escaping her conflicting emotions. Their relationship is complicated by other individuals. Mr. Solares, a wealthy Mexican who wishes to marry Mrs. Eastman-Cuevas, arrives with five wild female family members who have little regard for Gertrude's suffering. Lionel, a young man with a gloomy background, visits frequently and becomes attached to Molly. Also, Vivian arrives to spend the summer as a boarder with her widowed mother, Mrs. Constable, in tow. Vivian is an energetic, fun-seeking teen-ager who terrorizes and dominates her mother. She attempts to appropriate Mrs. Eastman-Cuevas' affections and tries to alienate Lionel's love for Molly, but she mysteriously falls off a cliff and dies, Molly being the only witness.

Two months after Vivian's death, a double wedding has taken place. Gertrude has married Mr. Solares, has moved to Mexico, and has sold the mansion. Molly has married Lionel, and they have settled at a nearby seafood restaurant. Molly cannot shake off her bondage to her mother and dreams of the time when she will return. Her mother, finding life intolerable among the Mexicans, does return. The crisis evolves out of Gertrude's unintentional confession to a homicidal act in which the circumstances were as mysterious as Molly's involvement with Vivian's death. Gertrude then realizes that her contempt and desire for ruling over Molly, as well as the identification of herself with her father, are all she has in her life. She tries to force the girl to leave her husband and live with her again; but Mrs. Constable, who has remained at the hotel in a dipsomaniacal state since the death of her daughter, manages to make the two recognize that the force between them is destructive, and so precipitates their final break from one another.

Henry Hewes felt that the play was a memorable one when

viewed as a study of neurotic unreality. But Harold Clurman found more ironic humor in the play and this feature, he felt, saved it from becoming overburdened with Freudian overtones. He remarked that *In the Summer House* could be called a "wryly comic lyric poem in a minor key," because the characters could be regarded as people isolated in a social world which exists statistically ("as a department store exists,") but not spiritually in a human context; and in that manner, "such people become weird—both sad and funny."[15]

Bowles' vision of life, capsulized in the characters of the two mothers, is indeed a mixture of comedy and drama, and her chief concern is with the two women: one ruthless and dominating who despises her passive daughter; the other, gentle and self-effacing who is dominated by her aggressive, uninhibited daughter. In spite of their differences, the relationships between the pairs are strangely interdependent. Henry Hewes suggested that the play gains in interest if Mrs. Constable and Vivian, the visitors, are thought of as alteregos to the first pair, Gertrude and Molly.[16]

Bowles approaches her main character, Gertrude, through psychoanalytical explanation. Her personality, it seems, is the complex chain of causes and effects, which Clurman attempted to summarize: the mother, being dependent on her father, has destroyed her daughter's will by re-enacting the father's role, thus causing her daughter to be mother-dependent; this explains nothing, said Clurman, but serves mainly to provide intriguing material for the playwright's exploration.[17] The convolutions of Gertrude's personality are dominated by her suppressed fears and are expressed through her dominating and aggressive behavior. Her own insecurity has originated with her love-deprived childhood. In compensation, she bolsters herself through self-deception and lies. In moments of introspection she reveals a persistent feeling of isolation, as if she had fallen off a cliff and landed miles away. She attempts to articulate the intensity of her aloneness but, in the process, realizes that even her griefs and sorrows don't seem to belong to her.[18] Nothing validates her existence and because this feeling frightens her, she retreats to the commonplaces of her life until her fears subside, just as her daughter finds refuge reading comics in the summer house. Rather than face her isolation, Gertrude finds a means to dismiss it.

Gertrude protests that her strength, like her father's, is her self-control. Never in her life, she claims, has she shown her feelings. Vivian's high-spirited behavior and uncontrolled emotional outbursts are despicable to her. She is even appalled by her daughter's awkward attempt to express her love for her. To Gertrude, human emotion is something dangerous. Startled by Molly's sudden flood of affection, she shows she is incapable of dealing with such feelings. This emotional aloofness is sponsored more from her deprivations than from the strength of her character. She has chosen as her model her father, who, in reality, loved her meek, frail, and delicate younger sister Ellen more than he did Gertrude. Having always sensed this betrayal, but having never faced it, she clings to the belief that he truly did love her.

But Gertrude's strength disintegrates when she loses contact with the false image of her father. Exhausted and insomnious, she returns from her disastrous Mexican honeymoon eager to free herself from the grotesquely comic Solares family. The incongruity of their credo, *joi de vivre*, which is pronounced happily by Mr. Solares with his heavy Spanish accent, is a hideous contrast to Gertrude's rules of self-control and self-denial. As a result of her chaotic life with the Solareses, she is unable to recall the standards and ideals which sustained her in the past. Again she deceives herself in believing that her life with Molly was full and happy and blames her dislocation on the Solares clan. Regaining possession of Molly is the solution to her dilemma, she thinks, but Molly's dependence on her mother's strength has been destroyed, and their relationship ends with Molly following her husband and with Gertrude's final admission to her true feelings of jealousy toward her sister and hatred for her father. The depths of the never-realized relationships between father and daughter and mother and daughter are made evident by implications that both Gertrude and Molly, out of their separate jealousies, caused the deaths of the individuals who threatened their illusions, Vivian and, presumably, Ellen.

The extraordinary effects of Bowles' psychological probing are heightened by a strong thrust of ironic humor. With this added dimension Gertrude can be seen as an eccentric character whose sharp and witty dialogue reveals the pointless and trivial aspects of her life. Thinking of marrying Mr. Solares has lead her to speculate about the behavior of Latins, those wholehearted individuals who enjoy living as much as she dislikes it. Speaking to Molly, but with her attention centered in herself, Gertrude parodies herself in a rambling continuous monologue which dominates the first ten minutes of the play. It is typical of the style which prompted Truman Capote to comment that the playwright's strange wit and sharp insight proved her to be an original, pure stylist.[19]

Bowles' "stylistics" extended into the haunting portrayal of the secondary character, Mrs. Constable, who was described by Eric Bentley as a memorable figure, defined by the commonplaces about dipsomania, spinsterhood and lostness, "yet coming together with the force of something new."[20] As the alter ego, Mrs. Constable is the reverse of Gertrude's dominating personality. In contrast to Gertrude, who has striking good looks and an imposing presence, Mrs. Constable is a frail, colorless individual who spends her days doing nothing because her life has been based on the pointless efforts to please an uncaring husband and demanding daughter. But, like Gertrude, she is confronted by the conflicts of gross reality and inner torment; rather than seeking to control them, however, as Gertrude does, she seeks release. After Vivian's death she speaks to Molly with a strange mixture of eloquence and pathos, telling her of the freedom she has found, but she never refers to the strange circumstances of the accident. Through alcohol she has extended and reinforced her release. Possessing the wisdom of the lost and exhibiting the uninhibited behavior of the inebriate, she provides another answer to human isolation, rebutting Gertrude's solution of finding solace in the trivial, that is, to wipe out all the petty details from her life.

Providing much of the pathos as well as "an exhilarating dash of rough comedy," Mrs. Constable serves also as a catalyst.[21] In a compassionate attempt to save Molly from the destructive obsession she has for her mother, she confides the "secret" of her escape from the memory of her widowhood and the death of her daughter: neither her husband nor her daughter had even belonged to her because neither had ever really loved her. When Molly realizes that the strength she admired in her mother, which she interpreted as love, "never belonged" to her either, she takes Mrs. Constable's advice and leaves with her husband.

Bowles' psychological approach is a striking contrast to Lorraine Hansberry's first play, *A Raisin in the Sun*, a realistic domestic drama which was produced in March, 1959, and won the Drama Critics Circle Award as the best play of the season.

There were many strong playwrights writing during the 1958-59 Broadway season, but, as Kronenberger noted, there was nothing fresh, new or vibrant about the works being presented; however, Hansberry emerged as a promising talent with her exceptional drama and became the first black woman playwright to have her work seen on a Braodway stage.

Proponents of the "new drama" called Hansberry's play a "throw-back to an outmoded style of dramaturgy," while traditionalists welcomed it as a return to "a more wholesome and intelligible era of dramatic writing."[22] Theophilus Lewis, drama critic for *The Catholic World*, held the latter opinion. He was relieved to find no "Freudian implication" in *A Raisin in the Sun*; it was straightforward social drama, he claimed, written in a refreshingly simple, naturalistic style.[23] Clurman called it an "old-fashioned play," even though he felt it showed some of the traits of the "new drama" in its moral fervor and "oblique lyric expression."[24] Hansberry, he opined, could not be considered a "neo-realist," however, because the play's inspiration was "less ambitious" and "more plainly specific"; Hansberry, he believed, simply wanted to say what she had seen and experienced, "because to her these things are sufficiently important in themselves."[25]

Despite critical arguments over its traditional form, *A Raisin in the Sun* was generally praised for its authenticity. Hansberry's portrait of the ambitions and anxieties affecting a black family living in the city was regarded by most critics as an honest response to a situation written by a knowledgeable playwright who had expressed herself profoundly. Richard Hayes declared that the Hansberry work presented a series of important implications to the playwriting field. First, it presented an emotional immediacy which rested on the playwright's perception of human feeling; secondly, it presented a tangible domestic realism anchored in traditional motive and psychology; and finally, in the playwright herself, certain characteristics were notable which were the play's vital source:

> [the play's] source must ultimately be the response to ... a spirit generous yet vehement, tough minded but without rancor; to a temperament able to contemplate experience with that uniquely unsexed, not sexless imagination of the very few.[26]

Both the playwright, Hansberry, and her play were all these things, Hayes stated.

Hansberry was a native Chicagoan, born in 1930 of an upper middle-class family. She studied painting at the Chicago Art Institute and the University of Wisconsin, and then found her way to New York. Working at various jobs before settling on writing as her life work, she met and married song writer and publisher Robert Nemiroff in 1953. *A Raisin in the Sun*, was completed in 1957. Through the efforts of small investors who had faith in the work, the play was tried out in New Haven, Connecticut, and then was produced in Philadelphia and Chicago before its Broadway opening in 1959. Two months later the play was awarded the Drama Critics Circle Award. Elizabeth C. Phillips in a critical commentary on the works of Hansberry noted that the granting of this award, in addition to recognizing the merits of her first work, involved other special distinctions: Hansberry was the fifth woman, the youngest playwright, and the first black writer to be granted it.[27]

Hansberry's specific concern rested with a black family's personal struggle to find its place. But a more universal concept provided a broader theme: the effect produced on human beings by continued postponement of a long cherished hope.[28] The play's title is an expression of this theme, and its explanation is found in Langston Hughes' poem "Montage of a Dream Deferred," which accompanied the published script. Hughes suggested that a dream deferred can dry up like a raisin in the sun; he ends his poem with the more disturbing possibility that the thwarted dream may even explode. Phillips commented that the allusion to the poem constituted an appreciable force behind Hansberry's title and was important to the articulation of the controlling idea of the play.

The plot focuses on Walter Younger, a young man who works as a chauffeur and, together with his wife and young son, lives with his mother and sister in a southside Chicago tenement. His dream is to escape the dreary existence he leads. When his widowed mother, Lena, receives a $10,000 life insurance settlement, he begins to make plans to go into partnership with a friend in the liquor business. But it is Lena's plan to buy a house for the family. There is conflict between mother and son, Walter and his pregnant wife, Ruth, and Walter and his sister, Beneatha, whose dream is to go to school and become a doctor. Lena makes a down payment on the house, which happens to be in a white neighborhood, in spite of her son's objections; but she gives the balance of the money to him for himself and for Beneatha's education. Walter foolishly gives the money to his dishonest partner. The proposed move to the new house is met with attempts by the white neighbors to persuade the family to stay out of their residential area. In a confrontation with the neighborhood representative the Younger family members assert their courage, in spite of Walter's troubles, realizing they can make a better life for themselves. Unifying their separate dreams and reconciling their differences, they go through with their plans to move.

Hansberry's play is a drama which emphasizes character. Although she presents her characters as victims of economic and racial inequity, she does not use them to indicate social reforms. As Lewis noted, she avoids crusading to correct social injustice, and, as a result, the characters do not have to prove anything. Simply presented, the characters are distinctive personalities, each one possessing individual personal motives. *Theatre Arts Magazine* noted that Hansberry's people were readily identifiable types, capable of gaining universal recognition and sympathy, but were sufficiently individualized to escape being nothing more than types.[29]

The real head of the household and perhaps the most outstanding character in the play is the stalwart matriarch, Lena. Her strength and integrity are the family backbone; it is from her sense of values and reverence for life that the rest of the family come to resolve their individual conflicts.

Lena's two most characteristic traits are her indomitable strength to endure hardship and her capactiy for human compassion. These are demonstrated in her dealings with her modern, headstrong children. She firmly defends her religious beliefs and demands respect for those beliefs from her agnostic daughter. Yet she is sympathetic with her daughter's ambition to be of service to mankind as a doctor. She rebukes her son's misplaced values, but her love for him is evidenced by her insistence that he is most in need of love when he least deserves it.

Hansberry invested in Lena some of the most moving passages of the play. Her uneducated, often homely dialect is simple, direct, and forceful, but carries with it poetic melody. To Walter's proposal that they accept money from the white neighborhood to stay out of their area, she retorts:

> Son—I come from five generations of people who was slaves and sharecroppers—but ain't nobody in my family never let nobody pay 'em no money that was a way of telling us we wasn't fit to walk the earth. We ain't never been that poor. ... We ain't never been that dead inside.[30]

Also, the disgrace of Walter's obsequious role-playing elicits a mournful, reflective response from her. But perhaps the most beautiful passage of the play revealing Lena's capacity for compassion is found in her denunciation of Beneatha's rejection of Walter.

> Child, when do you think is the time to love somebody the most; when they done good and made things easy for everybody? Well then, you ain't through learning—because that ain't the time at all. It's when he's at his lowest and can't believe in hisself 'cause the world done whipped him so. When you starts measuring somebody, measure him right, child, measure him right. Make sure you done taken into account what hills and valleys he come through before he got to wherever he is.[31]

An added dimension to her character is Lena's sense of humor. Her daughter protests that her varied preoccupations with horseback riding, guitar playing, and amateur acting are all expressions of herself. When Beneatha mocks Lena's pathetic little plant, a symbol of Lena's longing for space for things to grow, Lena defends its existence as a symbol which "expresses" her.

Lena's strongest attributes, her flexibility, strength, and love, ultimately instill in her family a devotion to her and a sense of unity with one another. Wisely she has raised her children to be strong-willed, but has also taught them, in spite of economic depravity and racial prejudice, to rejoice collectively in their good fortune and in life itself.

Attempting to characterize the 1959-60 season Kronenberger stated tht the success syndrome had become even more a controlling factor; high costs had created the "hit or flop" situation in which plays that were neither exceptionally good nor bad were automatically classified as failures. The belief that anything avant-garde, high-brow or special should seek success off-Broadway began to dominate the thinking of producers and backers; as a result one-third of the plays on Broadway closed within two weeks after their openings, and one-fifth of them closed within one week.[32] But Lillian Hellman's drama, *Toys in the Attic*, survived as one of the few Broadway plays to achieve success during this year. This play examined the relationship of two sisters and their dependent brother and the conflicts which ensue when he attempts to find an independent existence. According to Kronenberger, Hellman had "slapped a slumped, lethargic season into awareness" with this taut drama.[33] By this time the theatre had become oversupplied with dramas of the "new fiction" in which plot and structure had become less formal. In Kronenberger's estimation, *Toys in the Attic*, even though it emerged from Hellman's own experimentation with less structured style, helped to re-establish the concept that a play could present a plot with a destination.[34]

Toys in the Attic, one of Hellman's most substantial works, won the Drama Critics Circle Award for 1959-60. The insight and power of her earlier dramas were in evidence, but the influence of Chekhov was still prominent. From this influence Kronenberger noticed her sense of humanity seemed broadened through her more probing characterization even though she still possessed her "old mordant power."[35] She advanced, he noted, from human greed to human need, a far more universalized theme than that found in her earlier works.

Jacob Adler commented in the *Educational Theatre Journal* that Hellman modeled her drama after Chekhov's *The Three Sisters*, and from that work she learned to take no sides, urge no actions or attitudes as she portrayed the Berniers sisters in a situation similar to that of the Prozoroff sisters.[36] All of Hellman's previous plays, Adler noted, had been dramatically powerful through her vivid characterization, believable motivation, and clear, sharp dialogue; but, he concluded, her work seemed always too limited in theme and attitude for permanent value. *The Autumn Garden*, he suggested, was an attempt to expand her capacities as a playwright, but it seemed to miss her characteristic force; in *Toys in the Attic*, however, she was able to combine all her earlier strengths with compassion, truth, detachment, and dramatic power.[37]

The play's theme relates the ideas presented in *The Autumn Garden* and repeats the motif of human futility; but *Toys in the Attic* presents a fuller examination of the notion that individuals fashion their destinies by the accumulation of their acts and that dreams which are inconsistent with these acts are merely self-deceiving. Harold Clurman noted that the two sisters, Carrie and Anna, are upset by their brother's unexpected affluence because it threatens their hold on him; their dream of going to Europe and owning their house are merely "toys in the attic-playthings", used only by them as "psychological ornament."[38]

The story is laid in New Orleans. Julian Berniers is a likeable but irresponsible thirty-four-year old man who is protected by his two unmarried sisters. They adore their brother but they are upset by his marriage to Lily, a neurotic young heiress who is possessive of him and is content only when they have no money. All three women become distressed when Julian gets hold of some money in a mysterious way, buys them extravagant gifts and makes them wild promises about a financially secure future. The sisters realize that their hold on him has been weakened by his new independence, and

Lily is fearful that the money will change their relationship. When Carrie and Anna realize that their happiness will be destroyed by Julian's ostensibly successful business ventures, they discover ugly truths about their own symbiotic relationship. Carrie is revealed to have an incestuous feeling toward her brother, and Anna, recognizing her sister's viciousness in trying to get him back, becomes disillusioned and risks losing her sister's love by telling Carrie the truth about herself. Julian, after being brutally beaten and robbed as a result of Carrie's manipulations to hold onto him, eventually recognizes that he will always be weak and dependent.

The play is heavily plotted but conveys the same meaning as Chekhov's *The Three Sisters*, that, in spite of moments of insight, the characters will continue as they were before because people are as they are; like the Prozoroffs, the ultimate irony for the Berniers is that there is nowhere else for them to be but where they are.[39] Carrie already decides that nothing has happened when she rationalizes that "tomorrow is another day;" Julian's protest that he will not stay beaten is not convincing; and Anna gives up her courageous dream of independence to assist Julian and will eventually smooth out her relationship with Carrie and go on as before.

Hellman stated about the first draft of this play that she could write about men, but could not write a play that centers on a man. Her impulse was to write about the women around him, his sisters, his bride, her mother. Indeed, *Toys in the Attic* is centered in the author's interest in the helpless struggle of the two sisters who attempt to maintain purpose in their lives. Carrie's desperation leads to the grim and final downfall of her brother. The misfortune she precipitates, however, is not a result of pre-determined malefaction on her part, but comes from a blind compulsion to protect her own neurotic needs. Hewes claimed that in fact the real villains of the play were love, "in its most selfish aspects," and the human weakness to allow the need for it to consume others.[40] Carrie is a repressed woman who, by her childish desire to be pampered by Julian, becomes demonically possessive of him. She complains that he no longer pays attention to her since his marriage; she is hurt when his gifts seem inappropriate, even though he showers her with everything she claims she has always wanted: the mortgage to the house, a new piano, a trip to Europe. Her obsession has developed sub-consciously to the point of incest. When Anna is driven to telling her of this abnormality, she refuses to listen, but seeks devastating revenge. She renounces her love for her sister and cruelly informs Lily of Julian's past relationships with other women. Her intention is to destroy Julian's marriage and bring him back to her alone, but the implications of her actions are more extensive than she knows. She destroys the illusory basis of her life with Anna and reinforces Julian's status as a dependent failure.

Anna is a quiet woman who is able to recognize and face her own deceptions. She is a realist who knows her weaknesses. Refusing to gossip with Carrie about Lily's eccentricities, she comments: "I read somewhere that old maids are the true detectives of the heart. But I don't want to be a detective of other people's hearts. I'm having enough trouble with my own."[41] Like Carrie, though, Anna has based her existence on Julian's needs, but her love for him is not totally destructive. She is able to love without demanding that love be returned. Her maturity is evidenced by her strong sense of morality which overrides her personal wants. Her brother's irresponsibility is a source of concern to her, and she realizes that his business ventures are shady and need explanation.

But neither Carrie nor Anna want what they think they want or get. They both have fought self-realization by burying themselves in the details of their day-to-day lives and their excessive acts of self-sacrifice.

The 1950s were discouraging years for both male and female playwrights. It was an arid period in which the enterprise of play production was met with increasing costs and the fear of failure. These conditions had a dire effect on serious dramatists. By 1958 many of the plays produced had merely been processed for Broadway. As Kronenberger stated, no longer was the play the thing: "the show ... the stunt, the cut-down novel, the journalistic paste-up" seemed more attractive to financial backers.[42] In the popular sense, Kronenberger believed that there was nothing wrong with this; but he argued that there was a need to distinguish the production from the play, or "what is 'show business' from what is art."[43]

John Gassner observed that by 1960 the situation in the American professional theatre has worsened and was in serious economic and artistic straits.[44] The off-Broadway movement, however, which had begun to flourish during this time, exerted its strength by operating at low costs and was offering original and experimental works as well as revivals of the classics. Providing a hopeful alternative for unknown playwrights to have their works produced, the off-Broadway movement began to be seen as the underground mainstay of the legitimate stages.

Nevertheless, even though only four dramas by women survived production on a long-range basis on the legitimate stage during this decade, all four were exceptionally strong and compelling works.

Notes

[1]Lee Strasberg, ed., *Famous American Plays of the 1950s* (New York: Dell Publishing Co. Inc., 1962), p. 7.

[2]John Lardner, "The Theatre," in *The New Yorker*, 27, No. 5 (17 March 1952), p. 153.

[3]*Idem.*

[4]*Idem.*

[5]Walter Kerr, "The Stage," in *Commonweal*, 53, No. 26 (6 April 1951), p. 645.

[6]*Idem.*

[7]Lillian Hellman, *The Autumn Garden* (New York: Dramatists Play Service, Inc., 1951), III, p. 122.

[8]Euphemia Van Rensselaer Wyatt, "Theatre," in *The Catholic World*, 178, No. 1067 (February 1954), p. 386.

[9]Louis Kronenberger, ed., *The Best Plays of the 1953-54* (New York: Dodd, Mead and Company, 1954), p. 4.

[10]Wolcott Gibbs, "The Theatre," in *The New Yorker*, 29, No. 47 (9 January 1954), p. 54.

[11]Richard Hayes, "The Stage," in *Commonweal*, 59, No. 18 (5 February 1954), p. 449.

[12]*Idem.*

[13]Eric Bentley, "The Ill-Made Play," in *The New Republic*, 130, No. 2 (11 January 1954), p. 21.

[14]"In the Summer House," in *Theatre Arts Magazine*, 38, No. 3 (March 1954), p. 19.

[15]Harold Clurman, "Theatre," in *The Nation*, 178, No. 3 (16 January 1954), p. 31.

[16]Henry Hewes, "Broadway Postscript," in *The Saturday Review*, 37, No. 3 (16 Janaury 1954), p. 31.

[17]Clurman, "Theatre," in *The Nation*, p. 58.

[18]Jane Bowles, "In the Summer House," in *The Complete Works of Jane Bowles* (New York: Farrar, Straus & Giroux, 1966), I, i, p. 210.

[19]Truman Capote, "Introduction," in *The Complete Works of Jane Bowles*, by Jane Bowles (New York: Farrar, Straus & Giroux, 1966), p. 436.

[20]Bentley, "The Ill-Made Play," in *The New Republic*, p. 2.

[21]Clurman, "Theatre," in *The Nation*, p. 58.

[22]Theophilus Lewis, "Social Protest in 'A Raisin in the Sun'?", in *The Catholic World*, 190, No. 1135 (October 1959), p. 34.

[23]*Idem.*

[24]Harold Clurman, "Theatre," in *The Nation*, 188, No. 4 (4 April 1959), p. 301.

25*Idem.*

26Richard Hayes, "The Stage," in *Commonweal*, 70, No. 3 (17 April 1959), pp. 81-82.

27Elizabeth C. Phillips, *The Works of Lorraine Hansberry* (New York: Simon & Schuster, Inc., 1973), p. 16.

28*Ibid.*, p. 48.

29"A Raisin in the Sun," in *Theatre Arts Magazine*, 43, No. 5 (May 1959), p. 22.

30Lorraine Hansberry, *A Raisin in the Sun* (New York: The New American Library, Inc., 1966), III, p. 123.

31*Ibid.*, p. 125.

32Louis Kronenberger, ed., *The Best Plays of 1959-60* (New York: Dodd, Mead and Company, 1960), p. 7.

33*Ibid.*, p. 17.

34*Idem.*

35*Ibid.*, p. 18.

36Jacob H. Adler, "Miss Hellman's Two Sisters," *Educational Theatre Journal*, XV, No. 2 (May 1963), p. 117.

37*Idem.*

38Harold Clurman, "Theatre," in *The Nation*, 190, No. 10 (19 March 1960), p. 261.

39Adler, "Miss Hellman's Two Sisters," in *Educational Theatre Journal*, p. 117.

40Henry Hewes, "Broadway Postscripts," in *The Saturday Review*, 43, No. 11 (12 March 1960), p. 71.

41Lillian Hellman, "Toys in the Attic," in *Six American Plays for Today*, ed. by Bennett Cerf (New York: The Modern Library, 1961), II, p. 542.

42Louis Kronenberger, ed. *The Best Plays of 1957-58* (New York: Dodd, Mead and Company, 1958), p. 4.

43*Idem.*

44John Gassner, "American Theatre," in *The Oxford Companion to the Theatre*, ed. by Phyllis Hartnoll (London: Oxford University Press, 1972), p. 975.

Chapter V

1960-1970

The decade of the sixties was referred to as "the seasons of discontent" by Robert Brustein, a period which Harold Clurman claimed produced a "dramaturgy of the maimed," and was thought of as an "age of rubbish" by historian Richard Hofstadter.[1] The United States was involved in the strangest war of its history; social unrest, civil disobedience, overt left-wing activities, and public demonstrations for various social and political causes were witnessed as evidence of the uneasiness of the times. Nevertheless, reported Clurman, the theatre was healthy in its accurate representation of the society from which it derived its sources. The dramas produced, he asserted, were simply reflecting the causes and effects of such conditions and were truthful indicators of "an erosion of our sensibilities."[2] By the mid-1960s Otis Guernsey, editor of the *Best Plays* series, observed that on Broadway the number of serious plays dealing with serious subjects was "hardly worth mentioning" and that the comedies were presenting serious content but with irresponsible cynicism and irony which missed the larger issues at hand.[3] It was Guernsey's opinion that the preponderant comic form was failing to understand and take seriously an age which was beset with trying circumstances.

The schism between Broadway and off-Broadway had developed further, and the general impression of American theatre activity in the 1960s was that plays were being written and produced within a wide range of styles, themes, techniques, and forms. A total picture of the theatre of the sixties would include the conventional dramas of the Broadway stages as well as the activities of off-Broadway.

The contrast between the conventionality of Broadway and

the experimentation of the smaller theatres was striking and was reflected in the works of women playwrights during this time. Lorraine Hansberry's last complete drama, *The Sign in Sidney Brustein's Window*, was the only drama by a woman to reach a Broadway stage and run for over a month. Produced during the 1964-65 season, it followed the traditional three-act form and sought unity in tone and structure within the formal scene divisions of explication, conflict, climax, and denouement, the realistic characters undergoing a recognizable pattern of moral development. Hansberry's potential for further development was cut short, however, by her untimely death in January, 1965, at the age of thirty-four. *The Sign in Sidney Brustein's Window* had just opened in October, 1964, and was still running, although unsteadily, at the time of her death.

The history of the play's sustained run was dramatic in itself. The play had been met with indifferent response from the critics and had faced closure several times before its final performance. Believing in its message of idealism and hope in troubled modern times, and, as a tribute to the playwright, the cast, its producers, and several other interested individuals kept the production running for an amazing length of time considering the financial misfortunes and personal losses suffered. The battle to keep it open attracted much attention; committees were organized, discussion groups were held after performances, donations were offered, and other performers, playwrights, and theatre people offered their services to sustain its run. Guernsey noted that without this special effort on the part of its supporters, the play would surely have closed the week of its opening.

Most of the critics applauded Hansberry's intelligent writing and character perception, but the major negative criticism was that she had attempted too many plots. *Commonweal* critic Wilfrid Sheed stated that the play was a compendium of Greenwich Village legends: "the homosexual playwright, the junkie-prostitute, miscegenation blues—all jostling for equal time."[4] *Time* magazine reported that the drama seemed to have "too many minds of its own," that it was "overloaded, over written and overwrought."[5] The reaction of Harold Clurman was similar; he stated that Hansberry's work "suffers from sincerity. . . . She means to say *everything*."[6]

In retrospect, however, a critic for the *Village Voice*, Martin Washburn, asserted in May, 1970, that Hansberry's social insights had several far-reaching implications that were overlooked at the time the play was running. Seeing the play as a conscious "warning" to white liberal intellectuals to be prepared to confront "the spectre of black power," Washburn praised Hansberry's perception of this different social problem that was to explode less than a year and a half later.[7] On another level, Washburn declared, the character of the disillusioned Sidney was a warning to the younger generation of the late sixties which, as it aged, might find its values misplaced and its dreams jeopardized in ten or fifteen years, just as Sidney had.

Sidney's solution to his despair, Washburn noted, was derived from Hansberry's unfashionable yet uncompromising idealism, "the kind . . . [of idealism] we don't have anymore."[8] Hansberry believed in the ultimate goodness of people and Sidney, Hansberry's character with "sighted eyes and feeling heart," when confronted by the awareness of his own non-committed state, echoes Hansberry's belief that such an individual "cannot live . . . and not . . . react to the miseries which afflict this world;" the process of Sidney's re-awakening to his responsibilities to the human race conveys Hansberry's credo.[9] The playwright attempted to depict the pretentiousness of modern times through the disillusionment of not only Sidney's strata of society, the intelligensia, but through other levels as well: the bourgeoisie and the minority cultures, including blacks, homosexuals, and prostitutes. Her suggestion that the cure would be found through understanding, idealism, and common sense repeats the optimism of her first play, *A Raisin in the Sun*.

Sidney, a Jewish intellectual in his late thirties, lives with his wife, Iris, in their small Greenwich Village apartment. Both are frustrated in their professions. He is an unsuccessful nightclub-coffee house owner; she is a would-be actress with very little talent. Sidney is planning to embark now on another business venture, this time as editor and owner of a neighborhood newspaper. In spite of Iris' objections he takes on the responsibility of the publication and is persuaded by a local politician who promises to rid the neighborhood of corruption to support his candidacy. Sidney becomes an idealistic reformer and his efforts to help his candidate win are

victoriously rewarded. But Iris, unhappy with her unfulfilled aspirations and depressed by her job as a waitress, reveals to Sidney
the politician's dishonesty, then storms away in a bitter rage. Sidney, disillusioned, breaks down, gets drunk, and suffers from an
ulcer attack which he attempts to relieve with more alcohol. Iris'
younger sister, Gloria, a high-priced call girl, arrives, full of high
hopes of abandoning her life as a prostitute because she has become
engaged to Alton, Sidney's young, light-skinned black friend. But
Alton, upon hearing of Gloria's past, has left a letter with Sidney
telling her he cannot accept white man's "leavings." Gloria reads the
letter, and, when Sidney collapses on the sofa, she commits suicide.
Iris returns and both she and Sidney realize that they must learn to
face their inadequacies and heartbreaks realistically through a re-
affirmation of their love.

In spite of the critical consensus that Hansberry's play was
marred by disunity, her characters are distinctly drawn. Although
the play is centered in Sidney's struggles, Hansberry indicates a
sympathetic interest in the women of her play. The three Parodus
sisters, possessing the same family background but molded by different lifestyles and divergent ways, are appeciated for their complete development as human beings. All three rise above the limitations of their fixed roles of wife, mother, sister.

Mavis Bryson, the older sister, is a complex character despite
her well-defined position in society. She is introduced within the
context of her comfortable middle-class life and yet possesses a
basic honesty which enables her to view her own limitations. Sidney calls her The Mother Middle-Class, the embodiment of the middle class values against which both he and Iris have revolted. She
accepts this definition of herself, but not without a defense of her
way of life. She is shown to be something more than a representative of the uptown society in which she lives. Her wit and kindness
at the beginning of the play are indications of Hansberry's dissatisfaction with the philistine role which Sidney has designated for
her.

She has many prejudices which have been reinforced by her
marriage to her successful businessman husband, yet she is intelligent

enough to recognize them. In spite of her distrust of the Jewish race, she respects Sidney and incongrously feels comfortable in the atmosphere of his Bohemian home. But she cannot tolerate the thought of her younger sister being engaged to a negro. When she is introduced to Alton she is at first pleased that Gloria intends to marry such a strong, good-looking young man, but when she learns of his racial background she is mortified. This confrontation is a momentous event for Mavis:

> (She turns slowly around to face the youth again. It is a contemporary confrontation for which nothing in her life has prepared her. . . . For his part, Alton is prepared for virtually anything—to smile and kiss and be kissed; to scream or be screamed at, or to be struck and strike back. He is silent. Presently, this woman of conformist helplessness does the only thing she can, under these circumstances, she gags on her words so that they are hardly audible and repeats what she has already said.)[10]

However, Mavis' reaction to the rest of the group who have watched her embarrassment with smugness indicates another dimension of her character. As she begins to leave, taunted by the amused expressions on the faces of Sidney and his friends, she accuses them of having the same prejudices against "ordinary" people which she has against blacks. She tells them she would hope to find some understanding among those who call themselves intelligent artists and thinkers, for if people like herself cannot find understanding among them, then it can be found nowhere. Elizabeth C. Phillips, in *The Works of Lorraine Hansberry*, observed this as her parting shot to the atheists who have so effectually eliminated God for all other people so that the world has become, indeed, a comfortless place.[11]

Mavis' strength is expressed again during her talk with Sidney about her unfulfilling marriage. Seeking the admirable qualities she remembered in her father, a romantic who read classics and taught her Greek, she has married a man who she thought had those same qualities; but she was disappointed. By realistically accepting her role as neglected wife, she has been able to come to terms with her disadvantaged situation. Without self-pity she has refused the alternative of divorce not only for the sake of her three sons but also because she realizes that she cannot sustain a sole existence.

Gloria Parodus, the youngest daughter, is a fully realized character in spite of the potential for satire which is implied by her profession. As Phillips noted, ordinarily, although the prostitute is frequently encountered in literature, a contemporary call girl whose clientele is extremely wealthy would be treated satirically, but if the underlying thesis of the characterization can be accepted, that present-day society is too indifferent and merciless for the weak to cope with, then Gloria becomes "a genuinely pathetic individual."[12]

Most of what is known of Gloria is exposed by other characters since she does not enter until the last act of the play. Both Sidney and Iris, even though they have a genuine love for her, reveal their discomfort with Gloria's situation; in fact, it is their anxiety about her profession rather than Alton's racial background which makes them uneasy when Alton tells them of his intention to marry her. Their dialogue reveals their belief that Gloria is a victim rather than an aggressor in her profession and is a girl whom Sidney sees as not "tough" enough to survive in the world.

Gloria's physical appearance is not at all derived from the conventional image of the high-fashioned, big city whore. She is a young, wholesome, All-American type whose speech and manner suggest good breeding, even though in moments of high emotion she is betrayed by a coarseness in language.[13] She has a sensitive, kind nature, much like her sister, Mavis, which she reveals in her understanding of and sympathy for Sidney. Even so, her life has been brutal and coarse, but she holds great hope of quitting the kind of life which has led her to drugs, despair, and self-abnegation. She is honest in considering Alton's proposal of marriage, knowing that it is her way out but realizing that he must know of her past life before they marry.

She tells Sidney of the "rationales" with which she and the other girls buffer themselves against the harsh reality of their lives. These "rationales," noted Phillips, include all the cliches concerning the necessity of prostitution, and neither Gloria nor any of the other women, as Gloria has admitted, really believes in them. The thin protection afforded by these "rationales" is made obvious when Gloria reads Alton's letter. Unable to cope with the dissolution of her dream, she compensates by insisting that her past life would be better than dull marriage anyway. But her self-deceptive devices are futile, and when she is propositioned by David, the homosexual playwright, to participate in a perverse act with his latest boyfriend, she is unable to rely on the past rationales. It is at this point that she decides that death is better than a return to the degraded life she has known; invoking her father, who had denounced her when he died, she cries out for forgiveness. Her act of suicide, then, is an act of penance, and Hansberry's idealism, in spite of Gloria's helplessness and diminished alternatives, pervades even this, her most pathetic character.

Sidney's wife, Iris, is also invested with complex motives and unattainable aspirations. Physically she is attractive, younger than her husband, has an appealing personality, and a quick wit. Her most characteristic feature is her long, dark hair which, for Sidney, symbolizes her mixed ancestry and mountain background. The fact that her mother was Irish and had Indian blood and that her father was Greek sponsors Sidney's amused, yet proud remark that he is married to a Greco-Gaelic Indian hillbilly.[14] For Sidney, Iris has been the personification of his dream of a free mountain world where he is able to withdraw from the realities of the corruption, pollution, and materialism of his Greenwich Village life and renew his faith in the future. But Iris has gradually come to be dissatisfied with this role and longs to attain her own self-identity.

In an attempt to understand herself Iris has sought help from psychoanalysis. Realizing that her marriage is in a critical state and feeling the need to break free, Iris, however, uses her analysis as an excuse for her erratic behavior. Like Gloria's rationales, analysis has become her crutch made up mostly of superficial misconceptions and attempted justifications for her failures as an actress. Sidney, out of devastating honesty, cannot accept her reliance upon psychiatry and attempts to help her by pointing out her half-knowledge of the subject. But this only intensifies her growing antagonism toward him. In fact, the very quality that Sidney has found to be irresistible in her is the quality in herself which she abhors. She can think of her childhood as only provincial and stultifying, and Sidney's attraction to it encourages her frustration. Thus she seeks a more exciting life with a group of individuals whom Sidney calls "would-bes," those people who discuss their future successes but who lack the talent and integrity to make them happen. Her final capitulation comes when she accepts a job demonstrating hair curlers on television. Loathing the deceit involved and its degrading effects on her, she nevertheless defends the work because it pays a hundred dollars an hour. In retaliation for Sidney's cruel honesty and in the realization of her own shame and materialism, she proceeds to destroy Sidney's revived interest in human affairs by telling him the truth about his candidate.

Although some of her actions are destructive, Iris' love for Sidney remains constant. Phillips observed that at the end of the play when Iris recalls that her past life was filled with important relationships with her family members, particularly her little sister, Gloria, she finally becomes free to mature into the woman she had hitherto refused to become.[15]

The off-Broadway movement had attracted many writers by the 1960s and most of the activities of women dramatists during this decade took place in the small theatres, coffee houses, studios, and renovated buildings of off-Broadway. Adrienne Kennedy, Mary Drahos, Megan Terry, Barbara Garson, Elaine May, Rosalyn Drexler, Rochelle Owens, Myrna Lamb, Maria Irene Fornes, and Gretchen Cryer all produced works which ran for substantial lengths of time on off-Broadway or off-off-Broadway stages. The plays of these women belonged to what came to be designated as the "new" or "vanguard" theatre in which diverse media were combined with theatrical techniques to produce purely theatrical rather than verbal effects and in which audiences were invited to participate in the preponderantly improvised action.[16]

Henry Hewes remarked in his chronicle for 1963-64 that never in the history of the theatre had there been a time of so much controversy provoked by the American theatre as there was during this season. Indicating that the theatre had been "drifting into the doldrums of indeterminacy," Hewes stated that diverse opinion about what was happening on theatre stages at least gave vitality to the New York scene.[17]

The 1963-64 off-Broadway season marked Adrienne Kennedy's debut as a notable playwright with her strange and provoking drama, *Funnyhouse of a Negro*. Revealing a self-consciousness of her black race, Kennedy's work attempted to provide a new insight into racial issues by poetically exploring the private world of a sensitive, young negro girl who is surrounded by her nightmares of self-identity and is obsessed by fears of her cultural history and her past.

Kennedy, born in Pennsylvania and raised in Cleveland, began her college education at Ohio State University. As a black student, however, she found the social structure "so opposed to negroes," that she did little academic work while there.[18] She began writing when she was twenty years old and has written novels and several stories and poems, in addition to a number of plays. Her plays include *The Owl Answers, A Lesson in Dead Language, A Rat's Mass, A Beast's Story, Funnyhouse of a Negro*, and *Cities in Bezique*. Kennedy also collaborated with John Lennon and Victor Spinetti in presenting Lennon's book *In His Own Write* as a stage adaptation for Britain's National Theatre Company. The production was presented at the Old Vic, London, in 1968. She was awarded a Rockefeller Foundation grant in playwriting, and the New England Theatre Conference awarded her recognition for her playwriting.

Much of Kennedy's work is concerned with the problems of self-knowledge and identity and is pervaded by powerful imagery and "an intense desire to unite a self fragmented by opposing forces."[19] Indeed, this concern is articulated in *Funnyhouse of a Negro* through the figure of its main character, a miserable negro girl student whose hallucinatory world dominates the action of the play.

Funnyhouse of a Negro was originally presented in 1964 at the East End Theatre in New York; it was first published in 1970 in the *Best Short Plays* series and was selected by Stanley Richards, editor of the 1970 volume, as a truly innovative work of "fresh vision" and "pertinent advancement."[20]

The one act play, divided by blackouts into several scenes, depicts the last hours in the life of a young negro girl. There is little plot development since most of the action takes place in the mind of Sarah, the half-white, half-black writer-student who struggles with her mixed racial identity by imagining herself to be different personalities: Queen Victoria, the Duchess of Hapsburg, Patrice Lumumba, and Jesus Christ. Her nightmares occur in her small apartment which, to Sarah, has become a carnival funnyhouse where all things are false and distorted. Her conflict arises from the fact of her mother's gradual insanity and tortured death in an insane asylum and the illusion of her father's bestiality in seducing her mother. Mixed with her own guilt and confusion is Sarah's belief that white, symbolized by her mother, represents goodness, and black, personified by her father, is evil; and she is neither black nor white. In reality she has rejected her father and sometimes dreams that she has killed him by bludgeoning him with an ebony mask; other times she thinks he has committed suicide by means of the murder of Patrice Lumumba. While the figures of her imagination drift in and out as materialized beings of her subconscious mind, Sarah, unable to justify her existence in either a white or black world, commits suicide by hanging herself.

Generally reviews of the play were oblique, and some critics seemed confused by Kennedy's strangely constructed work. Edith Oliver from *The New Yorker* stated that the genre which the play suggested was one which, in her opinion, tended to make too much of small things (e. g., a character's inner torments and obsessions), but that Kennedy had managed to hold her interest and make her character's materialized nightmares seem important. She pointed out that Sarah, the central figure, was difficult to delineate since the dreams of her disordered mind dominated the action and the evidence of her character traits was relative to the twisted figures of her other selves.[21]

Critic John Simon, categorizing the play as a "psycho-drama," considered it to be an example of the negro "masochist play."[22] Likewise, Stuart W. Little, in his book *The Prophetic Theatre*, suggested that Kennedy's play personified a generation of blacks who were psychically confused about its heritage.[23]

Others, however, were impressed by Kennedy's poetic imagination and her ability to capture the essence of a distorted mind found in an entirely new context of the black experience. Richard Watts, Jr. wrote in the *New York Post* that he found Kennedy to be a remarkable writer "who may well possess a touch of genius."[24] Her most outstanding trait as a playwright, he remarked, was her "somber dramatic imagination" by which she was able to "weave a spell of phantasmagoric intensity" while exploring the recesses of a tormented mind.[25]

Gerald Freeman, who directed her later play, *Cities in Bezique*, for the New York Shakespeare Festival's Public Theatre in 1969, commented that Kennedy was an extraordinary poetic talent of the theatre. She did not deal in the traditional aspects of story, character and event, he stated, but in "image, metaphor, essence and layers of consciousness."[26]

Certainly the Kennedy play employed innovative techniques. The characterization of Sarah is deliberately cryptic. Several levels of identity are revealed so that Kennedy's main character, written to be played simultaneously by several persons, is a complex, and sometimes contradictory being who is never completely defined. Michael Anderson, an editor of *Crowell's Handbook of Contemporary Drama*, pointed out that this intricate interweaving of the parts of Sarah, in addition to Kennedy's stylized pattern of action, gave her plays the feeling of ritual, "pure drama freed from literal representation."[27]

All of the scenes are segments of Sarah's mental processes as she sits in her room contemplating suicide. The characters, culled from her imagination, embody parts of herself which are distinct from the individual the audience sees and hears as the "real" Sarah. In "reality," she seems to be a young person at first glance, but Kennedy reveals that at closer look she gives the impression of being ancient, boringly good-looking with no obvious Negroid features except for her head of frizzy hair. That feature is notable since she is obsessed with the notion that she is losing her hair. Indeed, part of Sarah's hair is noticeably missing, and she carries it in her hand. With the other hand she clutches a hangman's rope.

Directly addressing the audience she explains that part of the time she lives with Raymond, her boyfriend; and at other times as Christ, the Dutchess, and Victoria she lives with God, Maximilian, and Albert Saxe-Coburg. Her small brownstone apartment, her substitute place to be, is her theatre where her nightmare identities act out her fears, her funnyhouse wherein herselves exist.

The apartment is dominated by a grotesque white statue of Queen Victoria, her idol. It is a large terrible figure, possessing the quality of nightmares, suggesting probable death. Victoria tells Sarah of her royal world where everything and everyone is white and there are no unfortunate black people. Black is evil, reasons Sarah. Thus Sarah reveals that she is totally alienated from the world outside her mind and that she is unable to accept the reality of her racial history. She claims to place no particular moral value on her being and, in fact, wants nothing but complete anonymity.[28]

Sarah's inevitable path to suicide is traced through the actions of her imaged selves, and the imagery which the illusory characters create is central to the understanding of the meaning of the play. As devices designed to draw attention to certain characteristics of Sarah's nightmare world, such as the recognition of her oncoming madness, the disgrace of her mixed parentage, particularly her father's blackness which symbolizes evil to her, and her mother's mental and physical defilement, the four personages she has created are associated with Sarah's greatest conflicts.

Queen Victoria and the Duchess of Hapsburg, dressed in white satin and wearing headdresses and veils which only partially cover their wild, kinky black hair, look exactly alike. Their white faces are hard and expressionless and are still like deathmasks. Victoria is haunted by the fact that she is bound to the black Negro and must suffer her father's continuous visits to her even though he is dead. Her horrified reactions to the handfuls of hair which fall from her head symbolize and repeat the motif of Sarah's loosening hold on reality.

The imperial Duchess refuses to allow her father to return since she has refused all black men entrance to her chambers. She can escape her blackness, she says, since she is half-white, but her father can never escape his total shame. Scornfully the Duchess describes her father as an African "nigger," a Christian missionary teacher who is dedicating his life to the building of a mission in the middle of the jungle. Accusing him of defiling her mother, the Duchess hopes he is dead. It is while in the persona of the Duchess that Sarah carries on a sexual affair with the white man, Raymond, the funnyman of her funnyhouse, and it is to him she goes for refuge when chased by her father. As her hair begins to fall she cries to Raymond that she cannot be considered cruel in treating her father as an outcast for he has always been in the subservient posture of a grovelling menial to her.

The Duchess is visited by another of Sarah's selves, Jesus Christ, who represents a righteous justification for the spiritual murder of her father. Jesus screams at the Duchess to look at his hair which is falling out. They comb their hair together and become a hideous pair, both suddenly realizing that they are completely bald. Jesus cries out that he has tried to escape being black and that all his life he has believed his Holy Father to be God; but now he knows that his father is really a black man and he cannot deny his parentage. Thus, whatever he does, he will do in the name of God.

Sarah confronts her blackness in the figure of Patrice Lumumba, the black shadow which haunts her. He declares an intense description of himself and views himself as a vile and despicable representative of the black race.

The climax of Sarah's torment occurs when all four selves confront each other in the violent, overgrown jungle scene created by Sarah's mind. The characters wander about, speaking at once. Their speeches are mixed and repeated by one another, the noise finally reaching a climax as the figures rush about. They stop suddenly, standing still, then begin to chant of Sarah's bludgeoning her father. They end with a plea for Sarah's forgiveness and at that point Sarah hangs herself.

Several patterns and recurring images are found within the play by which Kennedy translates her continuous nightmare theme (the sins of the father's blackness are passed down to the daughter). The alternation of light (goodness) and darkness (evil) presents a chiarscuro of visual elements which symbolize Sarah's way of thinking. Sarah's selves are dressed in white; the scenes shift from Victoria's chamber which is bathed in a strong white light to the Duchess' chandeliered ballroom where snow falls on a black and white marble floor. The dark images support the quality of evil: black ravens fly abut the Queen's chamber and an ebony tomb-like bed is centered in the room. Raymond, who is white and for whom the real Sarah can feel no love, is dressed in black; and the last scene takes place in the wild black jungle grass which has overgrown the entire stage.

Also, the repeated motif of Sarah's hair is a graphic representation of the gradual deterioration of Sarah's grasp on reality. Fixed in her mind as evidence of her mother's dementia (the figure of her mother, who has straight, dark hair to her waist, wanders in and out, sometimes carrying her bald head in her hands), the symbol of her falling hair, which all the characters convey, indicates both Sarah's desire to be rid of her telling negroid feature and her knowledge that her mental world is collapsing.

The following season, 1964-65, the off-Broadway situation, according to Otis Guernsey, suffered from "internal indecision:" it lacked strong leadership; it had failed in its attempts to bring about a new identity; and there were no definite discernible trends among the new works.[29] Off-Broadway was marking time, judged Guernsey; nevertheless, it served its initial purpose by continuing in its efforts to assist new talent, especially at the small cafe theatres, the most productive being the Cafe La Mama. Viewed as a boon to new writers, these small theatres provided an outlet for such playwrights as Rosalyn Drexler, whose intentionally superficial and satiric short play *Home Movies*, produced in an off-Broadway house, was designated by the weekly newspaper, *The Village Voice*, as the most distinguished play of the 1964 off-Broadway season.

As novelist, actress, painter, and professional wrestler, Drexler has achieved recognition in many areas. She was a recipient of a Rockefeller grant in playwriting which enabled her to study theatre in Europe. Her novel, *I Am the Beautiful Stranger*, published in 1965, was described by the *New York Times* as one of the best books of 1965. She is also a member of the playwriting unit of the Actors Studio and is an original member of the Women's Theatre Council, along with Maria Irene Fornes, Julia Bavasso, Megan Terry, Adrienne Kennedy, and Rochelle Owens.

Home Movies, described by Henry Hewes as "concerning the carryings-on of a lot of strange people," indicates Drexler's penchant for satire, her off-centered humor, and bizarre point of view.[30] As a Greenwich Village attraction with its "patchwork of blasphemy and kooky quality," Drexler's first work created interest among the non-traditionlists of the theatre; this encouraged her to write other unconventional pieces such as *Hot Buttered Roll, The Line of Least Existence, The Bed Was Full, The Investigation,* and *Softly, and Consider the Nearness.*[31]

Richard Gilman, introducing a volume of her works entitled *The Line Of Least Existence and Other Plays*, points out that Drexler's most characteristic trait as a playwright is her irreverence for the orthodoxies of conventional art; this is reflected in her playwriting style, he suggests, which seems to ignore the rules of conventional theatre. "Appearance is everything and style is a way of living," is Drexler's motto, he states.[32]

The characteristics of her writing, that is, her emphasis on appearance on style rather than truths and hidden meanings, her use of langauge as bluff and guise which both lambasts the nature of language and points out its brilliance and wit, her assault on stultifying psychology, all convey her practical point of view of art. She has stated that she believes there is much more to fulfillment in life than creating a work of art. "I don't know if its's that important to create a work of art," she declares.[33] With this viewpoint Drexler allows herself the freedom to game-play as she writes. Gilman suggests that the name of the game might be "Keep them guessing," or "Never give a sucker an even break."[34] Her basic tenent seems to be that imposed rules and identifications should be repudiated and can be by outwitting the "identifiers and casting directors."[35]

Because the rules of her game are based upon the repudiation of superficial labels and categories, Drexler intentionally avoids searching for life's truths. All the truths she has to offer, Gilman claims, are contained in the appearance of her plays, the words and gestures she selects, and her imagination.

In plot, *Home Movies* consists of a series of farcical interludes by which the playwright satirizes surface morals, manners, and customs, and the false behavior of the people who create them. The play begins with Father Shenanagan, a lecherous priest who sings a Gregorian chant and plays the piano. Violet, the colored maid, pulls open the curtain to reveal Mrs. Verdun reclining in her bed wearing a lace peignoir and dazzling jewels. She and her daughter, Vivienne, a homely, eccentric spinster, talk of Vivienne's absent father and of Vivienne's compulsion to take her clothes off in public. Peter, a homosexual, arrives wearing several layers of clothing and talks of his attraction to the missing Mr. Verdun. Mrs. Verdun proposes that Peter marry her daughter; since Vivienne reminds him of Mr. Verdun, Peter agrees. Charles enters, a consumptive intellectual who communicates by whispering his lines to Violet, she in turn repeating them aloud. They talk of abstract matters while Vivienne unsuccessfully tries to undress. A truckman arrives and delivers a large closet to Mrs. Verdun who thanks him by attempting to seduce him. Mr. Verdun is heard singing from the closet and cries out for help to be let out. As Father Shenanagan and his companion, Sister Thalia, flirt with each other while catching cockroaches, Mr. Verdun breaks out of his closet and chases Charles away. The Verduns celebrate their reunion by drinking soup as Violet sings a blasphemous complaint that the Lord has done nothing for her. The other characters behave nonsensically as Mr. and Mrs. Verdun begin a wrestling match on the bed. Each sings a short verse and all end with the chorus: "Let no man now diminish/What takes two falls to a finish."[36] The actors then exchange roles and sing to each other.

This disjointed action suggests the title of Drexler's play. The family members and friends are seen momentarily in hilariously incongruous domestic scenes; they flit from one action to another like a badly spliced home movie. There is nothing more to her characters than what is seen in her rendition of split-second representation. Her characters, in fact, have been likened to the vague and funny images of the actors of the early silent films, with the addition of the sophistication of the Marx Brothers. Like those film comedians, Drexler's people are cheeky, willful, unpredictable, capricious, lordly and exist in a fantasy world which is set in conventional domesticity.[37]

Perhaps the most significant aspect of her characters is that none of them, true to Drexler's emphasis on appearance, is interested in the "meaning" of life, in moral truth, nor in social or psychological values:

> none is in lifelike relation to the others; none has a history or a future, a place to go after the play is over. They have all been invented only in order to rush madly around, armed to the teeth with language and also with the capacity to be quick-change artists, con men and false prophets, wolves in sheep's clothing and the reverse, so that they might do nothing else than establish an atmosphere of freedom . . . they make up new worlds of farce whose highly serious intention, as in all true examples of the genre, is to liberate us from the way things are said to be.[38]

Undermining several conventions of womanhood by means of her peculiar feminine characters, Drexler suggests that the imposition of roles and identifications upon women offer superb material for satire. Mrs. Verdun is described as "an imposing woman of grandiose proportions. . . . She enjoys herself and others, sexually and conversationally, although pseudo-religiosity is the operational framework."[39] Vivienne, the daughter, is a maiden spinster in her thirties. Presenting what appears to be a stereotype, Drexler immediately destroys the typical image by describing her as homely, zany, outrageously dressed and indecent. Likewise, Violet, the maid, denies typicality. She is

> a gorgeous supple beauty, completely at home in her surroundings. All desire her. She wears practically nothing: a top of feathery petals and a bottom of the same. Her long legs are encased in net stockings and her high-heeled shoes are spiked. Hooked to her bodice is a pom-pom, with which she occasionally dusts furniture and people.[40]

And Sister Thalia, the timid nun, appears in her proper nun's dress, but wears a platinum-blond wig under her wimple. Also she has a "crush" on Father Shenanagan: "Nervous as a little mouse. She is a refugee from an Eisenstein movie."[41] This "zany cabal" of women serves to demonstrate Drexler's intention, which is, as Gilman suggests, to liberate us from the way things are supposed to be.[42]

It was not until the 1966-67 season that another woman's work was to achieve long-running status. Megan Terry's *Viet Rock* was an exemplary expression of anti-war protest and epitomized the cause-pleading attitude of the year's off-Broadway season. As a series of vignettes which were directed by the playwright, the production made ironic social comment and presented adverse examples in a "persuader-device" of theatrical production.[43] Previously the trend had been for off-Broadway houses to rely on revivals of Albee, Beckett, Pinter, Ionesco, and Genet whereby directors seemed to be "merely toying with sensation"; but with such productions as *Viet Rock*, off-Broadway "went back to work," and attendance was greatly improved over seasons past.[44]

Viet Rock, a "folk war movie," developed from improvisations conducted by the playwright at the Open Theatre and indicated Terry's attitude toward experimentation in technique and subject matter and her interest in exploring political and psychological violence. Terry was born in Seattle in 1932 and received a B. A. degree at the University of Washington; she intended to teach school but abandoned that profession to seek a career in New York as a writer. Awarded a fellowship to Yale and a Rockefeller Foundation grant in playwriting, she developed as an innovative writer of the avant-garde, and her plays attracted several experimental groups, such as La Mama Experimental Theatre Club, the Open Theatre (she was a founding member of that organization), the Firehouse Theatre in Minneapolis, and several university drama departments. Besides *Viet Rock*, which was performed first in 1966, other plays include *In the Gloaming, Oh My Darling; Calm Down, Mother; Comings and Goings; Ex-Miss Copper Queen on a Set of Pills; Keep Tightly Closed in a Cool, Dry Place; The People vs. Ranchman;* and *Approaching Simone*. She has also written plays for National Educational Television.

First presented at the La Mama Theatre, *Viet Rock* was revised later for performance at Yale University and then was transferred to New York for its off-Broadway run. It was performed in several foreign countries as well. Phyllis Jane Wagner, who wrote extensively on Terry's works observed that *Viet Rock* was at first received overseas (particulary in Scandinavian countries) with more interest and acclaim than it was in the United States.[45]

Terry wrote *Viet Rock* at the height of United States' involvement in the war in Vietnam. She was one of the few playwrights who attempted to explore the anger in the country which evolved out of the war even though it appeared to be inevitable subject matter for socially conscious writers. (Harold Clurman thought that it was not surprising that the Broadway theatre had only tentatively explored the situation as dramatic material because in his view Broadway had become "understandably timid" in regard to controversial matters.[46])

Her works developed out of a series of improvisations which Terry had directed in the Saturday Workshop at the Open Theatre. Intended as a vehicle for the actors by which to explore new acting techniques, the production was formalized by Terry into a written script and prepared for public presentation by Joseph Chaikin and Peter Feldman.

In interwoven scenes the play focused upon the fate of seven soldiers, beginning with their births and culminating in their deaths. From the induction center where they are prepared to lead animal-like existences as soldiers, they are led to the battlefront in Vietnam and are conducted through such ritualized action as consorting with the native women, being shelled in their foxholes, and being deceived by the enemy. Meaningless congressional hearings are depicted, as well as back-home letter writing scenes between mothers and sons, sweethearts and recruits, all performed in loose, improvisational style wherein the ensemble of actors shift quickly from one scene to another.

Terry used a framework of folk rock music to accompany the series of improvisations as well as material derived from television and newspaper reports on the war and current vernacular for dialogue. It was intended that all the war cliches, including character types, would be exposed as indications of the meaningless action in which the country was involved. As representatives of individuals who were caught up in the war the characters emerged as stereotypes with the actors making no deliberate identification but rather exchanging parts from one episode to another. The sons, mothers, sweethearts, congressmen, soldiers of the Viet Cong were all depicted in a depersonalized fashion. Because it was the playwright's intention to explore a widespread public reaction to the war, her focus was centered in visual and emotional qualities rather than plot and distinct characterization. In her production notes, Terry explained that the acting ensemble attempted to deal with their anger and aggression over the war through personal stories acted out. Terry felt that it was important to explore their negative reactions, bewilderment, shame and confusion, then confine them to a form. From these exercises, she discovered that the visual images were more important than the words.[47]

Terry was interested in involving her audience with the results of her actors' exploration of their feelings against the war. She stated, "I want my audience to feel rather than think."[48] In reviewing her method of developing the formal structure of the play, she emphasized that she was intent on stressing an attitude of "light irony," building to "a certain driving ruthlessness" which, in her view, would express strongly the values of human inter-relatedness and mutual responsibility, thus drawing the audience in.[49] Terry declared that the value of the play rested in the fact that the problems created by war were universal since war and violence were apparently part of the national makeup. Admitting that the work grew out of current world events, Terry revealed that she had been berated by some of her fellow writers for "not writing something more timeless;" fortunately, she stated, these comments did not shock her into silence.[50]

Critical comment was extreme. Clurman appreciated Terry's propagandistic techniques but regarded the play as a disappointing attempt to arouse social conscience. He remained untouched by it and found "something peculiarly pretentious behind it all."[51]

Yale Daily News critic, Robert Bernard, observed that although Terry's humanistic impulse was admirable, the play seemed to be too negative, offering no real point of view nor any alternative course of action.[52]

But Richard Schechner, editor of the *Tulane Drama Review*, introduced the play as a theatrical innovation which furthered the cause of the avant-garde theatre movement. Terry's topical references, he believed, created the structure of her images and actions although these were conditional and transitory in comparison to the developments she had encouraged in the use of new theatrical techniques; for, in spite of the fact that *Viet Rock* touched a wide range of attitudes relating to the war, the play was non-political, not propagandistic, nor dogmatic, declared Schechner.[53] Its most important aspect was in its action. In fact, the play required that the actors confront and touch individual members of the audience. This was elegaic gesture to Schechner since it represented a real contact between audience and actor, the "theatre world and the worldly world."[54]

According to Schechner, Terry disregarded the rules and assumptions of the literary theatre of the past and thus achieved a technique consistent with the goals of the new theatre. Her work, he claimed, was a return to the playwright's original position as instigator of action, not merely creator of the written word. As a suggester of form, she organized the actor's spontaneous action which was derived from improvisation, then solidified it into a text subject to constant revision. Indeed, while working with the Open Theatre, Terry sophisticated her actors' quick-change improvising into acting "transformations," the device which Schechner indicated as Terry's most important contribution to the new theatre technique. By viewing her "transformations," the audience was forced to watch and interpret the action rather than focus on the personalities of the actors, characters, or playwright. The characters, situation, time, objectives and initial realities established at the beginning undergo a series of radical transmutations, these changes occuring quickly until, as Schechner noted, "the audience's dependence upon any fixed reality is called into question."[55] The effect was intended to be fluid, kaleidoscopic and explosive. Indeed, this effect was characteristic of *Viet Rock* because transformational figures are not intended to represent the minds of the characters or the playwright, but are used only to convey action.

The polarity of interests between Broadway and off-Broadway seemed fully apparent during the 1968-69 season. As a "season of transition," the year produced new theatre forms and new plays and playwrights at off-Broadway playhouses while at the same time uptown theatres continued to present conventional realistic drama and comedy.[56]

At this time two major trends emerged from both theatre fronts: an overt attempt to involve audiences and an explicit expression of sexual freedom. Guernsey noted that the stage was trying to make the most of its uniqueness which set it apart from motion pictures and television, the fact that the audience and the production were physically present together.

Actors were breaking down the illusory walls of realism by directly addressing their audiences and coaxing them to participate, even to the extent of inviting them to join them in free physical expression. This latter trend was found mainly in the smaller, experimental playhouses, and although it received more publicity than participation, it reinforced the notion that the theatre of the future could be a theatre of more direct contact berween play and audience, with the audience acting not just as isolated, passive observers but as active members of the production ensemble.

Concurrent with these trends was an upsurge of the number of productions which were given on off-Broadway stages. Compared with the 1967-68 figure of 72, 103 productions were offered; as Guernsey indicated, had it accomplished nothing else, the 1968-69 off-Broadway season distinguished itself by the large number of American playwrights who were given a hearing.[57] The best plays resembled the style, shape, and content of Broadway "hardly at all," and the movement was progressing in its function to serve as an alternate form of entertainment as well as to showcase new playwrights and plays.[58]

As a result of the interest in nudity on stage, sexual activity was more abundantly seen and deviations were not uncommon. Rochelle Owens' *Futz* exemplified this trend in women's writing. As an Obie award winner, *Futz* was cited as the best play of the 1968-69 off-Broadway season; it presented a man who enjoyed physical relations with his pig. In 1964 Lorraine Hansberry wrote of the inherent goodness of the human race, and *The Sign in Sidney Brustein's Window* was a thoughtful declaration that this quality could still be found in modern times. By contrast, Owens, in 1968, expressed a diametrically opposed view that man is by nature violent and that behind his acceptable social facade is a primitive animality, the very source of the physical energy from which his bestial violence springs. *Futz* was produced first for one performance at the Tyrone Guthrie Workshop by the Minnesota Theatre Company in Minneapolis, then by the Cafe La Mama Troupe at the La Mama Theatre in New York City in March, 1967; then it ran for six months in 1968 at the Theatre de Lys in New York.

The playwright, a native New Yorker born in 1936, is a poet and illustrator as well. Her poetry has been published in a 1962 volume, *Four Young Lady Poets*, edited by LeRoi Jones, and in *A Controversy of Poets* in 1965. A volume of her own poetry was published in 1968 entitled *Salt and Core*, and she has published and illustrated her book, *I Am the Babe of Joseph Stalin's Daughter: Poems 1961-1971*. Besides *Futz*, her most widely known plays are *Beclch, Istanboul,* and *Kontraption*. She also authored a full length play, *He Wants Shih*. She was recognized by the Rockefeller Foundation by a grant in 1965 in playwriting and by the Yale ABC Playwriting Program at the Yale University School of Drama in 1968.

Owens is a proponent of the "underground theatre" movement and insists that modern times require a new artistic response. Robert Schroeder, editor of *The New Underground Theatre*, classified her as one of a group of playwrights who contend that this era is so unlike any preceding time that art must shed its "constricting past" and experience a "complete rebirth."[59] Owens herself explained that her work encompassed "a fundamental and deep-seated human consciousness" which she felt needed no justification.[60] The most obvious proof of her rejection of established rules in her break with traditional forms such as that of the well-made social realism of Lillian Hellman and Lorraine Hansberry. Owens' reality, then, probes the psychic rather than the psychological. As a result her themes are bizarre and incongruous but express her support of the anti-tradition, anti-establishment revolution which seemed to have a profound effect on the non-academic artistic community of the 1960s. Schroeder also indicated that Owens' plays are commentaries on the sociological and psychological situation of modern America and reveal her interest in the chasm between man's "pretended aspirations" and his "pack-animal impulses."[61] This is the immediate and urgent dimension of the theatre which she sought in *Futz*. Her visceral appeal is indicated by her intense imagistic style.

Jerome Rothenberg, introducing the published version of *Futz* in 1968, described Owens' theatre as being a product of her own world; her consistent theme that man, for all his acculturation and sophistication, remains "the self-destructive animal—cruel-one of all our dreams and fears."[62] But Owens also sees man as the creator of love and, in this respect, perversity coexists with man's noblest dreams; man's cruelty to man is based in the tendency for human beings to be self deceptive in the process of conforming.

In *Futz*, Owens declares that man's sexual drives illustrate virtue as well as ugliness. Rothenberg positively assesses her central character, Futz, as "a man of-values, defender of all the grubby wonders of our flesh."[63] But critic John Simon in his review of the play reacted negatively to Owens' concept of man; he stated that even if one agreed with her theses that Futz' actions represented "the calvary of the non-conforming individual," her ideas, characters and even language were not dramatically legitimate, nor were they "couched in a dramatic event."[64]

A short play, *Futz* presents a rural American farmer, Cyrus Futz, who scandalizes his village with his overt sexual relations with his pig, Amanda. Enraged because Futz has spurned her in favor of his pig, the village whore, Majorie Statz, encourages her male family members to seek vengeance. Another character, Oscar Loop, has observed Futz with Amanda, commits a sex murder, and is hanged.

The Statzes create a furor among the villagers and persuade the authorities to imprison Futz; while in jail he is killed by Majorie's brother.

Sacrificing naturalistic characterization for an investigation into the realm of the irrational and depraved human psyche, Owens presents characters who inhabit a gross and obscene world. All of them appear to be deranged, demented, or perverted. Simon observed that not even Futz, ostensibly the only character with values, commands sympathy because, under pressure, he too proves Owens' man-as-beast thesis by cravenly denying his love for Amanda.[65]

And the human female is as animalistic as man, perhaps even more so since it is the jealously enraged Majorie who instigates the action of retribution against Futz and causes his death. Also, Oscar is hanged for attempting to rid the world of the wickedness he has just witnessed, its source being woman. Oscar's mother tells him that his act of murder was justified: "My son hates evil so he justly killed it. . . . That you should have killed an evil girl, is right. . . . No! Nobody—no woman is good . . ."[66]

Owens, attacking one traditional literary view of woman, that of "goddess," supports another by portraying her two main women characters, Majorie and Oscar Loop's mother, as predators. In Owens' world both men and women seem equally debased. Apparently Owens recognized that both views of women constituted a sexist attitude which, in her view, limited woman's "personhood" and "one's total humanity;" it was, she declared, the "Strindbergian" idea that man loves woman so much that he cannot live without her yet, at the same time he cannot live with her therefore he must hate her and put her in an inferior position.[67] But the playwright does not rescue her women from the "Strindbergian" curse; in fact, she reinforces the mythical notions that all women are predaceous (Majorie is dominated by one idea, revenge), and that even maternal love is self-seeking (Mrs. Loop comes to comfort her doomed son in jail and tells him that, after his death, the only thing that will be important to her is that her loving family must feel sorry for her because now she is a mother with no son). Furthermore, Owens presents Majorie as a physically repulsive figure. The Narrator describes her as about twenty-seven years old, "tall with square, worldly, insulted once maybe, body. Her coarse red hair is combed up in a sophisticated way which is sweetly silly in retrospect to her food-stained gingham, typical farm girl get-up."[68] Futz regards her as a "stinking human woman, disgusting girl,"while her brother calls her "the ole slot machine."[69] She is a burdensome tramp to her father who tells her, "Majorie, you're a poisonous snake. And if I didn't have to live in this village, I'd kill you myself. Your daddy or not—I hate you!"[70]

The image of the "godly" mother fares no better. Mrs. Loop, after telling her son that both he and she, in their roles as son and mother, are like deified beings, then instructs him that all women are inherently evil and are the cause of man's downfall. When Oscar gives her his only possession, some magical illness-curing spice seed insects which he calls life's essence and which can make dead things come alive again, she proves her point by greedily grabbing them to cure her arthritis, then flings them into the air, oblivious to the fact that they might have saved her son.

But Owens' women are not the only objects under attack. All mankind, being human, is sub-normal, and in Futz' non-conformist view, which apparently reflects the playwright's, being animal is the highest achievement since animals are incapable of the devious actions by which man attempts to subjugate his fellow man.

The 1970-71 season off-Broadway presented only a modest display of skill even though it was characterized by "considerable variety."[71] At this point the off-Broadway movement seemed susceptible to, and receptive of, the effects of civil and social unrest; it was at this time that Myrna Lamb's *The Mod Donna*, a protest of women's liberation partisans, was produced. An experimental "rock lyric" play, it reflected the theatre's increasing interest in the issues of the women's liberation movement of the 1960s. Focusing her attention on the personal frustrations of contemporary American women, Lamb raised the issues of women's liberation in a persuasive indictment of mutual exploitation in marriage.

By the late 1960s the activities of political and social groups organized to further women's legal and political rights had influenced the cultural front as well as social and political thought. The offensive side of the question of the new women's movement provided inspiration for several women writers to explore the situation in modern terms, not merely reflecting the effects of the movement, but becoming part of its development as well.

As a comparatively new playwright and as a representative of this new school of feminist playwrights recently emerging, Lamb wrote a series of plays under the general title, *Scyklon Z, A Group of Pieces with a Point*, which dealt with the problems of the contemporary movement. Some of these sketches became popular attractions of various theatrical organizations and reform groups. Her short play, *But What Have You Done for Me Lately?*, was staged by the New Feminist Theatre in 1969 as part of a program investigating abortion in New York City. It depicted, in a sex-role reversal, a male character who against his will undergoes a fetal implantation. His plight is complicated by his frustrated efforts to obtain help and sympathy for his condition. The play was presented again at the New York Socialist Workers Party 1970 Campaign Kick-Off Rally. A new scene was added in which a trial was held with the audience as jury to hear the man's case. After viewing Lamb's graphic demonstration of sexual exploitation of women by men, the audience-jury verdict, integrated into the action of the play, rendered the man an unfit parent, and voted that the pregnancy be terminated.

The anger with which Lamb viewed social ills that directly affected women, refined and sharpened in her longer work, *The Mod Donna*, was indicated by the subtitle of *But What Have You Done for Me Lately?*, "Pure Polemic"; in fact, Lamb's intention was made even clearer by her introduction to the play in which she explained her rage at having to deal in secret with her teen-aged daughter's suspected pregnancy. She admitted frankly that her purpose in writing the work was to present a diatribe, "a piece of agit-prop."[72]

The most notable example of Lamb's unquestionable attitude was *The Mod Donna*, or "A Space-age Musical Soap Opera with Breaks for Commercials," one of the first feminist theatrical events to achieve widespread recognition. The play was produced by the

New York Shakespeare Festival Public Theatre, May, 1970, directed by Joseph Papp. In *The Rebirth of Feminism*, authors Judith Hole and Ellen Levine point out that as of 1970 there was no widespread feminist activity within the professional theatre and *The Mod Donna* was one of the earliest theatrical events of its kind to receive significant public attention. The Papp production was to serve mainly as a "consciousness raising" function. As such the play was not designed to create more or better jobs for actresses, women directors, playwrights or technicians; but the feminists involved hoped to arouse the awareness of both theatre people and of the theatre public to feminist issues.[73]

Lamb specified that her play was a modernized version of wife-swapping founded in the traditional *menage à trois* situation, and, in this instance, it becomes a grim, discordant travesty of domestic life. The main plot involves two married couples: Jeff, the boss, and his wife, Chris, the "haves;" and Charlie and Donna, the "have-not" underlings. The "boss couple" are elegant in dress and life style while their counterparts, the "have-nots," take the role of the likeable "all-American" couple who exude innocence, hope and idealism.

The plot is a deliberate soap opera parody. Donna seeks happiness in a *menage à trois* with her husband's boss and his calculating wife. The employer's wife, Chris, has set up the situation hoping to revitalize her husband's sexual interests in her. When she decides that the relationship has served its purpose and is to be terminated, the now-pregnant Donna refuses to agree. Chris gives Donna's husband, Charlie, an album of photographs which show Donna and Chris' husband in various illicit sexual activities. But Charlie refuses to challenge his boss and places the blame on his wife, whereupon Donna points out her own debasement and humiliation. Enraged, her husband threatens to kill her; Donna shouts that she will not be a human sacrifice for his manhood. But the play culminates in Donna's symbolic execution as the chorus sings a bitter song of liberation.

Critical reaction to the play was divided. *Time Magazine*, Clive Barnes of the *New York Times*, and Natalie Gittelson of *Harper's Bazaar* all favored the work as a lucid and stimulating view of modern male-female relationships. On the other side, *New York Times* critic Walter Kerr, and *Newsday's* George Oppenheimer felt that Lamb's work was merely a puritanical, anti-sex lecture. And Dick Brukenfeld, reviewer for *The Village Voice*, took an ambivalent stand. Praising the playwright's courage and wit, Brukenfeld nevertheless found little satisfaction in the story which, for him, proceeded by logic that was neither masculine nor feminine, "just dangerous"; Lamb had intended to show how sex could become a destructive force in human relations but in creating her work, she had allowed a philosophy which saw culture as the only determining factor in her characters' lives.[74] Railing against the fact that people make objects out of one another for their own pleasure, Lamb had done nothing to mitigate the problem she has posed and, in fact, had created her four characters as objects, said Brakenfeld.[75] But the strongest feature of the work, he declared, was the playwright's anger, and, in spite of what he saw as oversimplifying propaganda, he felt that Lamb explored a "relevant, often inflammatory sector of current reality," which, he claimed, "won't leave you complacent."[76]

Vivian Gornick rebutted *all* reviews of the play in her *Village Voice* evaluation, stating that even the sympathetic criticisms were inaccurate and that everyone seemed to have missed Lamb's point. The real driving force and theme behind Lamb's presentation, asserted Gornick, was woman's imposed and self-imposed obsession not with sex, but with sexuality, the obsession with her own desirability that powers all her actions, and her rage at having no other means by which to define herself.[77] Gornick believed that although Lamb was an unpredictable writer and, so far, one with only "partial control," her work was stabilized by emotional truth and self-awareness, qualities that were only just beginning to show themselves in Western culture as the true totality of the feminine mind; thus, in her view, Lamb was the "first true artist of the feminist consciousness."[78]

The playwright wrote a polemic against American marriage as an introduction to the published version of *The Mod Donna*. In it, she stated that marriage was "a fitting punishment for the ... obscene reasons for its existence."[79] Believing that the liberation of woman was the ultimate revolution encompassing all those that had come to pass in the past century, Lamb declared that for both men and women to support it meant that the male of the species might also be liberated, that he might be "freed forever from supermasculine compulsion," to join the female "in full and glorious humanity."[80] Depicting marriage as "the sad seesaw," Lamb intended that her play show what had happened to human beings in marital relations in a society in which people avoided truth and denied true feelings.[81]

Accompanied by rock music, a chorus of women provided an interspersion of "commercials," plays-within-the-play, which supported Lamb's views and commented upon the main action. The chorus was to be comprised of women from varied races and ages but the playwright designated that it should also appear to be androgynous. As an integral part of the production, the chorus moved, sang, and philosophized.

Some of the playlets sharpen Lamb's polemic. "Charlie's Plaint" is the cuckolded husband's lament that even though he exerts power over the office secretaries, receptionists, and typists, he has lost face with his wife and so has lost his masculinity. In "Pannassociative" the chorus sings that the ideal wife fills her husband's needs by becoming his non-demanding sidekick. "Astociggy" depicts a women's march to the concentration camp, followed by a scene called "Planned Obsolescence for Women." But the most powerful interlude, entitled "Beautiful Man," is a stunning retort to pornographic abuses of women, and is, as Gornick suggests, "the most marvelous parody of Mailer-esque male pornography imaginable, and given life by the double turn-about of obvious female pornography it alludes to."[82] In it the chorus describes a public rape-ritual of a virgin by a stalwart and virile fantasy male-figure. The chorus follows with an ironic refrain which praises the "beauty" of the rapist.

The entire action of the play results from the stratagems and manipulations of the two women, Chris and Donna, the purposely stylized figures who are drawn to demonstrate human action rather than to reveal individual patterns of behavior and personality. Both are motivated by sexual disillusionment. In spite of the ostensible dominance of Chris, who conceives the idea of the triangular arrangement and who seems to tyrannize both Donna and her own husband, the women share the "contemptible dilemma" of being female.[83] When Chris suggests to her husband that they incorporate Donna into their marriage, it is her last attempt to revitalize her relationship with him. And as Donna's symbolic execution by her outraged husband begins, a member of the chorus steps forward to reassure the audience that Donna has been raised since birth to accept herself as a sacrificial lamb. Like the ritual-rape of the previous scene, the sacrifice of Donna and the manipulations of Chris are witnessed and justified by a society that the playwright sees as encouraging male supremacy while restricting feminine identity. Both women act upon each other and their mates with the ironic hope that "sexual manipulation will somehow end sexual definition."[84] But, as Gornick points out, the more devastating irony is that both are helplessly tied to this grotesque situation because sexual definition *is* their precise and ultimate definition. Neither one is free to escape, and neither one has the ability to walk away from the whole affair. They are both caught in an "exhausting circle of fear, jealousy, self-hatred and isolating competitiveness" which will continue for the rest of their lives.[85]

The chorus finale presents Lamb's undeniable message at the conclusion of the play:

> They tell us we are bound by grave and gravity
> Yet we must beat ourselves against the stone
> The tablets of a prophet of depravity
> The rock is fathergod oppressor grown
> Let them tell fields to be fruitful for the nation
> Let us not be compliant earth to willful seed
> Let us cast another god from our true vision
> Our true need
> LIBERATION   LIBERATION   LIBERATION[86]

In spite of the unsettled times and conditions of society during the 1960s, or perhaps because of these circumstances, this decade was one which resulted in an abundant expression of a variety of themes by women playwrights. The social unrest in the United States during this time provided a background for women's overt expression of opinion and reaction to their changing roles in a changing society. Reflecting the trend for new playwrights to seek recognition, many women playwrights availed themselves of the opportunities to experiment and innovate on the less commercially-oriented stages of the small off-Broadway and off-off-Broadway stages. The last Broadway success to be studied here, Lorraine Hansberry's *The Sign in Sidney Brustein's Window*, can be viewed as a traditional drama in spite of its interjections of anti-realistic scenes when compared with the psychic probing of Adrienne Kennedy in *Funnyhouse of a Negro*, the study in aberrant sexual behavior in *Futz* by Rochelle Owens, and the social protest explored by Megan Terry in *Viet Rock* and Myrna Lamb in *The Mod Donna*.

Notes

[1]Harold Clurman, ed., *Famous American Plays of the 1960s* (New York: Dell Publishing Co. Inc., 1972), p. 13.

[2]*Ibid.*, pp. 13-14.

[3]Otis L. Guernsey, Jr., ed., *The Best Plays of 1966-67* (New York: Dodd, Mead & Company, 1967), p. 6.

[4]Wilfrid Sheed, "Theatre," in *Commonweal*, 81, No. 7, p. 197.

[5]"Theatre," in *Time Magazine*, 84, No. 17 (23 October 1964), p. 67.

[6]Harold Clurman, "Theatre," in *The Nation*, 199, No. 13 (2 November 1964), p. 340.

[7]Martin Washburn, "Theatre: The Me Nobody Knows," in *The Village Voice*, 15, No. 22 (28 May 1970), p. 45.

[8]*Ibid.*, p. 46.

[9]*Idem.*

[10]Lorraine Hansberry, *The Sign in Sidney Brustein's Window* (New York: Random House, 1965), I, ii, p. 63.

[11]Elizabeth C. Phillips, *The Works of Lorraine Hansberry* (New York: Simon & Schuster, Inc., 1973), p. 98.

[12]*Ibid.*, p. 99.

[13]Hansberry, *The Sign in Sidney Brustein's Window*, I, i, p. 5.

[14]*Ibid.*, I, i, p. 14.

[15]*Ibid.*, II, i, p. 76.

[16]Clurman, *Famous American Plays of the 1960s*, p. 15.

[17]Henry Hewes, ed., *The Best Plays of 1963-64* (New York: Dodd, Mead & Company, 1964), p. 3.

[18]Stanley Richards, ed., *The Best Short Plays, 1970* (New York: Chilton Book Company, 1970), p. 127.

[19]*Idem.*

[20]*Ibid.*, p. xiii.

[21]Edith Oliver, "Off Broadway," in *The New Yorker*, 34, No. 49 (25 January 1964), p. 76.

[22]John Simon, *Uneasy Stages* (New York: Random House, 1975), p. 185.

[23]Stuart W. Little, *Off Broadway* (New York: Dell Publishing Co. Inc., 1972), p. 233.

[24]Richards, *The Best Short Plays*, 1970, p. 127.

[25]*Idem.*

[26]*Idem.*

[27]Michael Anderson and Jacques Guicharnaud, *Crowell's Handbook of Contemporary Drama* (New York: Thomas Y. Crowell Company, 1971), p. 271.

[28]Adrienne Kennedy, "Funnyhouse of a Negro," in *The Best Short Plays, 1970*, Stanley Richards, ed., (New York: Chilton Book Company, 1970), p. 133.

[29]Otis L. Guernsey, Jr., ed., *The Best Plays of 1964-65* (New York: Dodd, Mead & Company, 1965), p. 26.

[30]Henry Hewes, ed., *The Best Plays of 1964-65* (New York: Dodd, Mead & Company, 1965), p. 365.

[31]*Ibid.*, p. 10.

[32]Rosalyn Drexler, *The Line of Least Existence and Other Plays*, with an introduction by Richard Gilman (New York: Random House, 1967), p. ix.

[33]"Five Important Playwrights Talk About Theatre Without Compromise and Sexism," in *Mademoiselle*, 75 (August 1972), p. 386.

[34]Drexler, *The Line of Least Existence*, p. x.

[35]*Ibid.*, pp. x-xi.

[36]Rosalyn Drexler, "Home Movies," in *The Line of Least Existence and Other Plays* (New York: Random House, 1967), p. 118.

[37]Drexler, *The Line of Least Existence*, p. ix.

[38]*Ibid.*, p. xi.

[39]Drexler, "Home Movies," p. 77.

[40]*Ibid.*, pp. 77-78.

[41]*Ibid.*, p. 78.

[42]Drexler, *The Line of Least Existence*, p. xi.

43Otis L. Guernsey, Jr., ed., *The Best Plays of 1966-67* (New York: Dodd, Mead & Company, 1967), p. 29.

44*Idem.*

45Megan Terry, *Approaching Simone*, with an introduction by Phyllis Jane Wagner (New York: The Feminist Press, 1973), p. 35.

46Clurman, *Famous American Plays of the 1960s*, p. 18.

47Megan Terry, *Viet Rock and Other Plays* (New York: Simon and Schuster, 1966), p. 21.

48"Theatre," in *Time Magazine*, 88, No. 17 (21 October 1966), p. 61.

49*Idem.*

50Terry, *Viet Rock*, p. 22.

51Harold Clurman, "Theatre," in *The Nation*, 203, No. 18 (28 November 1966), p. 587.

52"Theatre," in *Time Magazine* (21 October 1966), p. 61.

53Terry, *Viet Rock*, p. 17.

54*Ibid.*, pp. 17-18.

55*Ibid.*, p. 10.

56Otis L. Guernsey, Jr., ed., *The Best Plays of 1968-69* (New York: Dodd, Mead & Company, 1969), p. 3.

57*Idem.*

58*Ibid.*, p. 28.

59Robert J. Shcroeder, *The New Underground Theatre* (New York: Bantam World Drama, 1968), p. vii.

60"Five Important Playwrights Talk About Theatre Without Compromise and Sexism," in *Mademoiselle*, p. 289.

[61]Schroeder, *The New Underground Theatre*, p. ix.

[62]Jerome Rothenberg, "Introduction," in *Futz and What Came After* by Rochelle Owens (New York: Random House, 1968), p. vii.

[63]*Idem.*

[64]Simon, *Uneasy Stages*, p. 143.

[65]*Idem.*

[66]Rochelle Owens, *Futz and What Came After* (New York: Random House, 1968), p. 23.

[67]"Five Important Playwrights Talk About Theatre Without Compromise and Sexism," in *Mademoiselle*, p. 386.

[68]Owens, *Futz and What Came After*, p. 6.

[69]*Ibid.*, p. 20.

[70]*Ibid.*, p. 21.

[71]Otis L. Guernsey, Jr., ed., *The Best Plays of 1970-71* (New York: Dodd, Mead & Company, 1971), p. 30.

[72]Myrna Lamb, *The Mod Donna and Scyklon Z* (New York: Pathfinder Press, Inc., 1971), p. 143.

[73]Judith Hole and Ellen Levine, *Rebirth of Feminism* (New York: Quadrangle Books, 1971), p. 370.

[74]Dick Brukenfeld, "Off-Off," in *The Village Voice*, 15, No. 19 (7 May 1970), p. 53.

[75]*Idem.*

[76]*Idem.*

[77]Vivian Gornick, "Who is Fairest of Them All?" in *The Village Voice*, 15, No. 22 (28 May 1970), p. 47.

[78]*Ibid.*, p. 50.

[79]Lamb, *The Mod Donna and Scyklon Z*, p. 7.

[80]*Ibid.*, p. 28.

[81]*Ibid.*, p. 16.

[82]Gornick, "Who is Fairest of Them All?" in *The Village Voice*, p. 50.

[83]*Idem.*

[84]*Idem.*

[85]*Idem.*

[86]Lamb, *The Mod Donna and Scyklon Z*, p. 139.

Chapter VI

Summaries and Conclusions

Have women dramatists, then, been able to define what their characters are in terms of what has given shape to their own lives, as something *sui generis*, rather than follow forms and themes which have been traditionally based on the conventional point of view? By tracing the achievements of women playwrights throughout each decade, some responses can be drawn which indicate certain trends in the development of the American woman playwright from 1930 to 1970.

Summaries

During the 1930s the predominant themes explored by these representative playwrights appeared to be mainly social and domestic themes in which comedy, farce, drama, and melodrama were employed. The economic depression in the United States created general deprivations in the theatre but it was countered by two satiric works which pointed out the foibles and shallownesses of upper class American society. Clare Boothe's *The Women* was a scathing attack on the private lives of the women of the Park Avenue set in New York City. A milder satire was levelled against the superficialities of the wealthy in Rachel Crothers' *Susan and God*. By contrast, in *Another Language*, Rose Franken dealt with the domestic adjustments of a middle class family and attempted a serious consideration of a woman's non-conformity in a traditional family situation. A new playwright emerged among women writers with full force. Lillian Hellman probed abberrant psychology in *The Children's Hour* and was launched as one of America's outstanding playwrights. At the same time traditional historical romance found outlets in

Susan Glaspell's *Alison's House* and Zoe Akins' *The Old Maid*. At the end of this era a stronger national consciousness was evident in Lillian Hellman's examination of the roots of the evils of industrialization and exploitation of the south found in *The Little Foxes*.

This period was closest in time to the passage of the Right to Vote amendment which gave impetus to woman's participation in almost every field and occupation. However, because the broader goals of the feminist movement were achieved with the passing of the amendment, the awareness of women's rights seemed to lose momentum, and the effects of dominance-oppression in male-female social problems remained much the same even though there had been a great change in manners and morals as evidenced before by the "flapper" era. Women did not seem to be writing plays in protest for certain rights, as Rachel Crothers did years before in her fervid questioning of women's achievements outside the home, that subject being the basis for several of her earlier works such as *A Man's World* (1909) and *He and She* (1911). There was little of the young Crothers' feminist stand in the plays of the 1930s. This might be indicative of the idea that these playwrights were not necessarily committed to the cause of finding a voice with which to express feminist grievances. However, the subsiding of the feminist movement was no indication that the social problems of women had been alleviated, and women writers at least seemed aware of the unresolved questions which remained for women in American society. This is evidenced by their subject matter. Such topics as lesbianism, illegitimacy, marital infidelity, maternity, and the social alienations of non-conforming women were included.

All of the playwrights representing this decade drew their material from the situations of women in various times and societies in environments which traditionally focused on man's place in society. In fact, women characters predominated in the women's plays of this era. The action of each play examined focused on the relationship of woman to her family, society, or history, or on the relationship of one woman to another.

In *Alison's House* Susan Glaspell emphasized the feminine perspective by paralleling the personal struggles of a woman of the present with similar conflicts of a woman of the past; the title of Rose Franken's drama, *Another Language*, referred to a young woman's stance for her own way of life against that of a cruder, family majority's. Lillian Hellman, who claimed that the theme of *The Children's Hour* was the destructive forces of a lie, nevertheless centered the conclusion of her play on the ruinous consequences in the lives of the two women who had been defamed; in *The Little Foxes* she concentrated all the evil tendencies of a greedy family into one character, a female, Regina, around whom the action revolved. *The Old Maid* presented Zoe Akins' obvious concern with the outcome of a continuous competitive relationship between two female cousins. Rachel Crothers focused attention on the evaluation of priorities in a woman's life in *Susan and God*. This orientation reached its climax in this decade with the all-female cast of thirty-six characters in Clare Boothe's *The Women*.

As evidenced by the central position which women held as characters in these plays, it may be concluded that the playwrights shared an interest in women's lives, and, in some cases, most evident in the dramas of Lillian Hellman, there was an attempt made to explore deeper ranges of women's psychology and inner motivations.

The Children's Hour, for example, presented two levels of the playwright's consciousness: her awareness of the forces of society in relation to individuals, and her investigation into the personal reaction to those social forces. In general the critics understood her social moralizing but were confused by the last act. The consensus of critical opinion was that Hellman "tagged on" an ending to *The Children's Hour* by fixing her attention on the relationship between Martha and Karen. The majority of critics believed that the play would have been sounder dramaturgically if the play had ended either with the eventual triumph or the ultimate downfall of the child antagonist. This criticism might have defined the playwright's technical failing, it seems, but it did not take into account the playwright's apparent need to explicate a situation, peculiar to women, whose definitions had not been understood, even by the women themselves. Indeed, Martha suggests that the love of women for women has no name; it has been dismissed as a subject about which women have never been allowed to think or talk. It might be suggested that Hellman included the last act confessional between Martha and Karen because apparently she was concerned about one woman's struggle to define what kind of love she was allowed to feel for another, thereby suggesting that it has been every woman's struggle. Since there is no recognition of that condition of woman's relationship to woman either on the part of society or that of the protagonists themselves (for they are conditioned victims of that society), it is regarded by both as equivalent only to what is recognizable, the illegitimate and scandalous practice, lesbianism.

Hellman, as well as other playwrights of this time, attempted also to evaluate the variation in roles found in woman's social standing. She revealed the social position of Karen and Martha to be predicated on assumptions and hidden prejudices about unmarried women who seek independent careers. The exemplary lives the two have led count for nothing when the lie affirms society's suspicions about them, and the astounding rapidity with which the lie is accepted as truth indicates the force of pre-judgment. By contrast, in Hellman's *The Little Foxes*, the impulse behind Regina's power-hunger is precisely her own belief in the mediocrity of her social position. Rather than a victim of her society, as Karen and Martha are, Regina is its product.

Zoe Akins drew a striking contrast between Delia, the stylish, well-to-do girl who values social standing and prestige, with the humility and simplicity of Charlotte, her impoverished cousin. Because of her social advantage, Delia is able to manipulate the fate of Charlotte whose future is restricted by her position as a middle-class dependent. The controlling factor in Charlotte's life which has forced her to play the role of "poor relation" has always been her lack of financial security. It is that which prevents her from establishing a life of her own and reclaiming her illegitimate daughter.

Rose Franken presented the variation of roles from a different angle in *Another Language*, but the contrast between characters was similarly dramatic. Although all the Hallam wives come from the same strata of society, one of them, Stella, does not fit the pattern from which the others have been molded. The others are dull, insensitive, and gossipy. Stella is not. They are complacent in the monotony of their marriages; Stella strives to overcome the common-places which are creeping into hers. Although the middle class social standing is shared, Franken pointed to the possibility of two different roles which could and did emerge.

Clare Boothe seemed to suggest in *The Women* that there may be differences in social roles which women play between upper and middle classes, but basically all women strive for the same objective (at least in her satire): the desperate pursuit of men.

But in spite of the centrality of women characters in these plays, the playwrights of the 1930s alleviated the problem of the stereotyped woman character in their literature to only a small degree. Most of the major characters considered come to predictable futures. Boothe's play, *The Women*, for example, is made up entirely of what the author referred to as satiric types. The basic concern of the play is with sex; the characters' lives are completely determined by how long they can hold onto their men, and their only means of survival under these conditions are the maintenance of youth and attractiveness of their bodies. Even the protagonist, Mary Haines, representing the "norm," is predictable in her well-ordered marriage and finally in her reliance upon familiar feminine trickery to win back her husband.

In *Allison's House,* Elsa is condemned for assuming the initiative of creating a life of her own despite social censure; and Alison, her plantom alter-ego, received praise for passively accepting her fate of living alone. Passivity has a higher value because it is presumed to be the expected female mode of behavior. Alison, in death, is regarded by the other male *and* female characters as an exalted super-human, a transcendent poet-goddess, esteemed not only for her genius as a poet, but for her conventional behavior; Elsa is considered base, weak, and pitiably human.

An aggressive woman such as Hellman's Regina in *The Little Foxes* who succeeds in adopting the male quality of self-assertion, is considered unfeminine. Hellman concedes to this by indicating that elder brother Ben is constantly amazed by his sister's lack of feminine softness. He advises her that she could further her cause by using more subtle, feminine persuasion.

Rachel Crothers created her character, Susan, in *Susan and God*, as a woman whose search for logicality continually leads her through meaningless pursuits with preposterous goals. In this way Crothers seemed to reinforce the notion that a woman's intelligence is often equated with her "mysterious" intuitive powers; thus Susan's thought patterns seem fuzzy and flightly in spite of her high level of intelligence.

A reversal of this attitude was found in *Another Language* wherein the materialism of the wives and mother of the Hallam clan is viewed in a negative sense when compared with the idealism of Stella. But Stella is viewed by the others as a misfit since her idealism is considered non-utilitarian in the domestic routine of a woman's role. Franken recognized this as the inequity of a social cliche, but, rather than condemn the practice, she accepted it as a device for drawing her stereotyped wives as background for Stella's conflict.

But, to some degree, the playwrights did attempt to perceive certain types as being three-dimensional individuals, and, in some measure, these characters were endowed with some control over their own destinies. Several of the works studied from this period suggested that the idea that women must accept their biological destiny as being their sole function in life for the good of men and children and for their own sakes as well is in opposition to a part of woman's nature which, when thwarted, results in conflict. Stella, the heroine of *Another Language*, has chosen her role of "submissive wife," enjoys it, and is willing to be subordinate to her husband; but she rebels against the diminishing effects of a marriage defined by middle-class values. Her ideas of being a "good wife" are frustrated by her unwillingness to give up her freedom to be herself in exchange for the role she is expected to play as a member of the Hallam family. Paradoxically, this is her strength as a human being but her defect as a family member. By actively challenging the family values, she produces a change in her husband; and even though her purpose in life is still to be the submissive wife, she will play the role for a different kind of husband.

Charlotte, the "old maid" of Zoe Akins' play, plays her role with the specific purpose of hiding her instinctive maternal urges toward her daughter. As an "old maid" she submits to all its implications: she is an observer of life, not an active participant; her small joys come from vicariously living others' experiences. She changes her appearance to reinforce the part she plays, wearing her hair severely pulled back and dressing in plain, dark clothing in contrast with Delia's colorful, fashionable appearance. Her manner is brusque, business-like, and fussy. But she is not an absurd caricature of proverbial wasted feminity. She is drawn out of pathos and great sympathy and her life is not deprived of human feeling. She courageously forgives the mistreatment she has suffered at the hands of Delia; finally, and more importantly, she finds the strength to forgive herself.

To label Regina from *The Little Foxes* merely a "dominating wife" would be to overlook the nuances of a study of distorted personality which Hellman created. To be sure, Regina has all the characteristics of this type of woman: unnaturally she dominates men, depriving them of pride (her brothers) and virility (her husband), then despises them for the weaknesses. But Hellman probes further to reveal the causes for Regina's need to dominate (which are explored even further in the antecedent play, *Another Part of the Forest*). She exposes Regina's hateful childhood in which male children were prized above females.

Thus, the bewilderment of female identity in various societal backgrounds was indicated in most of these works. It seemed to be from a male standard that most of the women characters were drawn, but it was also the confusion derived from that standard which formed the major conflicts in the characters' lives. This might suggest that the women playwrights of this time were not necessarily searching for re-definition, but that they were expressing the confusions in roles which resulted from a society which declared that the characteristics of men were the norm. Although they attempted to extricate the problems of their women characters, the playwrights seemed not to have described their characters by any other means than the male norm standard. The characters were placed in the conventional feminine attitudes, the predictable ones, passive, intuitive, materialistic, possessive, being the most characteristic.

The conclusions of the plays reflected the irresolution of this problem of woman's struggle for freedom of choice in a male world; the answers that were proposed were often based upon dramatic expedience. For instance, Elsa remains society's outcast at the conclusion of *Alison's House*, with only a private redemption experienced through her aunt's poems. Franken's conclusion to *Another Language* appears to be a compromise of Stella's idealism. The sudden conversion of her husband to her way of thinking leaves the question: how long will his change of attitude last? And how effectively has the victory been in the battle against family tradition? *The Literary Digest* argued that the playwright's expedient resolution was spurious since the curtain falls "with the lady still in chains," and the insensitive nature of her husband remains fundamentally unchanged.[1] Hellman outlined a bleak future for the surviving school teacher, Karen, in *The Children's Hour*. Bereft of the will to be part of the society which condemned her and which now vindicates her, she has few inner resources left to help her reassemble the pieces of her shattered life. Karen exemplifies human futility and ultimate passivity, attitudes to which she has by now been thoroughly conditioned. Therefore, she meets the conflicting realities of her situation in a predictable manner: she does nothing. This is the "lack of spiritual development" seen by Wyatt, the *Catholic World* critic, who pointed to this void as the reason why *The Children's Hour* "just missed" being great tragedy.[2] In *The Old Maid* Charlotte's unhappy life is resolved by a magnanimous act of Delia's in which Charlotte's daughter is urged to include her in the mother-daughter talk which is to take place the night before the daughter's marriage. Mary Haines' triumph over her ex-husband's wife is shallow, but is the expedient upon which Boothe relied to conclude *The Women*. Mary wins the right to wear the symbolic "Jungle Red" nailpolish, and thus armed for battle, joins the ranks of her peers to fight for her survival in tht female world. In *Susan and God* the solution to the problem of Susan's search for her life's purpose is in her domestication. And Regina in *The Little Foxes*, perhaps the most liberated character of all those studied, ends with the fear of being left alone.

The women playwrights of the 1930s presented both negative and positive views of women in the roles of wives, mothers, old maids, divorcees, and career women. Although writing from traditional bases, they showed a persistent awareness that in some ways the conventional roles themselves were the source of conflict for women who desired greater fulfillment from such roles. Generally, the characters analyzed are antisocial in that their search for freedom of choice is at odds with the society in which they live. From them is demanded compromise if they are to survive. But the playwrights, even though exploring the conflicts, offered no more substantial resolutions than more sacrifice on the part of their women to adjust to the demands of their paternalistic societies. In some instances, such as in *The Children's Hour* and *Another Language*, the adjustment is not favorable.

Throughout the 1940s changes in themes and roles occurred in women's playwriting. American women playwrights were influenced by the prevailing commercial, industrial, and economic conditions brought about by World War II and the post-war period. A situation developed which directly affected women writers. During the war, women at home were encouraged to work in almost every occupation to replace the men who had been called into the armed services. At the outset of World War II the theatre became a more receptive place for many women writers since the reservoir of male talent was being depleted by war enlistment. And subject matter was affected also. Many of the topics with which women dealt were centered in timely, serious problems concerning the nation in general. Yet, of the nine serious plays by women that were popular during this decade, five could be considered as woman-centered in which an interest in women's lives was expressed as central to theme; they were Rose Franken's two plays, *Claudia* and *Outrageous Fortune*, Elsa Shelley's *Pick Up Girl*, Fay Kanin's *Goodbye, My Fancy*, and Carson McCullers' *The Member of the Wedding*.

Both Franken dramas were thoughtful investigations of personal tragedy in the lives of women, *Outrageous Fortune* being a candid exposure of various social ills as well. Shelley presented a strongly realistic re-enactment of a day in New York City's Children's Court in *Pick Up Girl* in 1944. Pointing to the increase of juvenile delinquency in a war-time society, Shelley anticipated the post-war difficulties of readjustment among American youth, particularly young girls, and exposed an immediate problem that had few satisfactory solutions. Two post-war pieces, *Goodbye, My Fancy* and *The Member of the Wedding*, presented women as central characters in search of complete identity.

More general themes were presented by the remaining four playwrights. Hellman extended her political ideologies and led other dramatists to probe the causes and effects of world war. Using the troubled political scene as background for her equally troubled characters, she presented two successful dramas between 1940 and 1945, *Watch on the Rhine* and *The Searching Wind*. In 1942, Sophie Treadwell's drama of social values, *Hope for a Harvest*, emphasized some of America's neglected domestic problems. It underscored the waste in human character as paralleled with the deterioration of the once fertile land of the California valleys which had been exploited by loafers and commercial opportunists. Treadwell's sincerity and idealism were perhaps the most outstanding aspects of her drama.

From 1945 to 1950, only three serious works by women authors were presented continuously on Broadway stages. They were *Another Part of the Forest, Goodbye, My Fancy*, and *The Member of the Wedding*. This apparent decrease in serious works by women seemed to indicate the current trend of thought in which it was felt that the vacancies that women were called upon to fill during the war were now to be made available to the returning men; for women, attention was directed back to their responsibilities of building families and re-establishing homes. Many women who wrote seemed to be relegated automatically to minor status. The more serious writers seemed easily discouraged by the increasingly limiting "success syndrome" of legitimate stage producers and backers who were more willing to finance the seemingly surer successes of light comedies and musicals. Therefore, many of the women playwrights who remained in the professional theatre scene wrote in the comedic vein, generally avoiding themes of war. Led by actress Ruth Gordon with her second play, *Years Ago* (1946), this group became commercially prosperous with plays that were intended mainly to amuse. Two prominent comedy writers were Mary Chase (*Harvey*, 1944) and Anita Loos (*Happy Birthday*, 1946). The trend toward domestic comedy in women's writing continued throughout the 1950s with plays such as *Gigi* by Anita Loos and *Mrs. McThing* by Mary Chase (1951-52); Mary Chase's *Bernardine* (1952) and Jean Kerr's *Mary, Mary* (1960) continued the tradition.

In the plays of the 1930s which have been examined in this study it was found that woman's social standing was of great importance in determining female modes of behavior in dramatic characterization. In the earlier plays emphasis was placed on the predicament of women who were caught between the dictates of impersonal social forces and their own personal needs. In the plays selected from the 1940s less role variation was found from one economic class to another mainly because most of the female protagonists of these dramas, with one exception, were representative of the comfortable middle class or wealthy upper class. The exception was found in *Pick Up Girl* in which Elizabeth, coming from a destitute, struggling New York City family, typifies the case of the wayward ghetto child. The fact of her economic background is, as the playwright implied, precisely the cause of Elizabeth's delinquency. And because her social position is determined by her poverty, she is deprived of controlling her own fate when her actions are judged as antisocial by the law.

However, most of the other female protagonists represented the high middle class and upper income strata of society. From these advantaged positions most of these women characters come to their individual situations either well-educated and well-traveled, or at least financially secure. Rose Franken's Claudia leads an idyllic life; her husband, a successful, young architect, has provided her with every comfort, including the exclusivity and charm of an old farm home. She has enjoyed the pampered life of being the only child of a remarkably liberal and loving mother, and her husband has attempted to continue the kind of life to which she has been accustomed.

Sophie Treadwell indicated that although her character, Carlotta, the disillusioned woman of *Hope for a Harvest*, returns home destitute, her education and experience living abroad have given her the spiritual substance with which to begin a new and productive life for herself. Her inherited homestead is run-down, but vestiges of a past elegance remain, indicating Carlotta's aristocratic background. She is willing to rebuild her security to regain the dignity of her family name; her poverty does not limit her hopes.

In Hellman's *The Searching Wind*, Cassie and Emily circulate within the privileged society of diplomats, celebrities, and sophisticates, and both enjoy the freedom of the wealthy class. Within that society their actions are neither condemned nor condoned, and the two women are free to pursue their private interests while maintaining their positions in society.

Crystal Grainger of *Outrageous Fortune* lives a mysterious life in which her social standing is often questioned but is more often envied and inevitably admired. She has made her own rules of behavior and lives and dies by them. In fact, her last unconventional action before she dies is a gesture of seduction; it is an overt act befitting her social defiance, but true to her singular nature.

In *Another Part of the Forest* Regina's position is determined by whoever holds the family purse strings, and, when the power struggle between Ben and her father results in Ben's conquest, Regina's loyalties shift easily. That she is controlled by the possessor of the family wealth is Regina's limitation, but she is shrewd in accepting her subjugated position, knowing that power can be obtained elsewhere. She agrees to Ben's demands that she marry a wealthy man for whom she cares nothing because she recognizes that their father's money will never be shared.

Agatha Reed in *Goodbye, My Fancy* leads the somewhat fantasized life of a liberal, intelligent, glamourous female politician who, as a post-war ideal, is a self-contained woman, making her way in life through honest effort and integrity. Her social prominence cannot be jeopardized by society's conventional image of woman because she represents society's highest values.

Perhaps the most dramatic contrast which illustrates woman's variation in social roles was presented by Hellman in *Watch on the Rhine* in the mother-daughter relationship of Fanny Farrelly and Sara Mueller. Sara, who has given up the luxurious life of the

American upper class for a life of poverty with her German husband and children, confronts her mother, who is the obvious representative of the Washington elite. Fanny understands little of the life Sara has chosen to lead and less of her reasons for not asking for help when she needed it. But she does understand her daughter's values. They share equal stature on that basis in spite of the diametrically opposed directions of their private lives. Indeed, the indomitable spirit of the mother has been passed on to the daughter as the basis for Sara's unwavering convictions. Neither the privileges of the wealthied class nor the deprivations of the poor have compromised this integrity.

In general the women characters examined in these plays reflected an ambivalent place in society which women had obtained as a result of wartime economics. Having to meet the demands made on them to join the work force in support of the war effort, women were offered more opportunities for careers, education, and travel which broadened the scope of their experience. Kanin's protagonist was a Congresswoman; Hellman's figures were embassy wives and mistresses, underground participants, and wealthy, willful daughters. Rose Franken dealt with a notorious seductress image as well as the eccentric personality pattern of a child-bride. Sophie Treadwell depicted a highly educated, worldy-wise woman of distinction whose dignity overcame her poverty.

Yet at the same time that women characters were being placed in new roles outside the home, their personal worth was judged by their authors by how stable their relationships were with the dominant male characters. In spite of their estimable positons which enabled them to achieve on their own, these characters, it seemed, could not remain autonomous; or, if they did, they suffered great losses. Crystal Grainger staunchly upholds her life of "outrageous fortune" and moral freedom, but dies. In *The Searching Wind* the inevitable conclusion drawn regarding Cassie's liaison with her best friend's husband is that her illicit relationship could not be based on love or genuine affection but must hide a baser motive: Cassie's femininely competitive desire to punish her rival. As Hellman indicated in the broader political theme, immorality is punishable and Cassie must suffer through an agonizing self-appraisal which leaves her contemptuous of herself. In *Another Part of the Forest* Regina is propelled even further into a state of depravity when she shifts loyalties from father to brother and feels no regret for her father's pitiable position. Sara's nobility in *Watch on the Rhine* is recompensed by the loss of her husband to a cause which has always been greater than her own personal needs; and Carlotta in *Hope for a Harvest* must risk losing the companionship of Elliott when she disregards his prejudiced advice. Claudia's situation is resolved when her mother-dependency, a trait no longer tolerable in a married woman, is transferred to David, who, as her protector-husband, is a more socially acceptable recipient.

But perhaps the most vivid example of this ambiguity was the character of Agatha Reed of *Goodbye, My Fancy*; Agatha, in spectacularly surpassing every standard of success which she has encountered, is the concrete expression of American moral, social, political, and economic achievement. But because her life lacks a male counterpart, her personality is unfinished. By expedient manipulation on the playwright's part, the most likely mate being eliminated because of his non-committal politics, Agatha's personal crisis is relieved by her attraction to the transient and glib *Life Magazine* photographer.

It seems apparent from these dramas that there was no open challenge to the fundamental attitudes about women's place in society even though in reality many women were filling positions left vacant by the conscription and enlistment of men for the service. Most efforts to explore the changes that had taken place in women's lives as a result of the war were tentative and irresolute. The persistent attitude that, in spite of woman's proven adaptability to and compatibility with work outside the home, she should subordinate her career to the ultimate goal of home and husband was crystalized in *Goodbye, My Fancy*. The superwoman achievements of Kanin's "liberated" Congresswoman are thought of by the character as incidental; her "true" womanly nature demands male companionship and a family in order to be complete. The play ends predictably with Agatha finding a man, but her choice seems irrelevant since it is merely a convenience to resolve Agatha's "half-existence" as a single woman, even though she is an extraordinarily successful single woman.

Nevertheless, a continuity of thought can be found in the plays of women of the 1940s which indicate some universal problems. Even though the solutions to the problems are not always similar, the ways of female feeling appear to be consistent in their presentation. In several of the plays the emphasis was placed upon woman's search for escape from existing conventions. This generally is seen by the character's desire to go somewhere other than where she is at the present. Hellman revealed this in all three of her plays. It is found in *Another Part of the Forest* in Regina's desire to run away and ingratiate herself into the social world of Chicago. To Regina, Chicago represents freedom, and her obsession to go remains with her even in middle-age, as is seen in *The Little Foxes*. In a more complicated situation, Hellman's participants in the *affaire de trois* of *The Searching Wind* (the title itself indicating this theme) pursue each other from one international location to another in the attempt to resolve the complexities of their relationship, but their globe-trotting only increases the confusion. In *Watch on the Rhine* Sara has a subliminal desire to recreate the happy times she spent as a child in her parents' home and returns to her homeland after twenty years with the vague hope of finding solace for her family. By creating such a contrast between Sara's background and her present situation, Hellman personifies the theme of the suffering and placelessness of the European war refugee as compared to the security and plenty of the American capitalist.

Treadwell, Franken, and Kanin all utilized the motif of women attempting to adjust to their circumstances. Like Sara, Treadwell's Carlotta returns home after many years of living abroad. She is attempting to escape rootlessness and the fear of being alone since the outbreak of the war in Europe and the death of her husband. She returns, physically and mentally exhausted, hoping to make a new life for herself in the California valley. Similarly, Crystal Grainger, Franken's heroine, flees from a complicated world, but her escape is motivated by her wish to find a peaceful place to die. She finds it at the Harris' shore home, but also fulfills another purpose in helping to ease a tense family situation. In *Goodbye, My Fancy* Agatha's escape to her college days results in an unexpectedly negative experience since Agatha's peace of mind cannot be found in reconstructing the past but rather in living the present. Unlike

Crystal, whose escape is not only productive in straightening out the lives of others but also fulfills her wish to die in peace, Agatha's retreat "back to the womb" is unrealistic and falls apart because it works against her natural ability to face life squarely. When she recognizes this inconsistency she is able to resume active participation in life.

The same flight from reality was seen in adolescent behavior by Shelley and McCullers. Shelley depicted the ambivalent struggle of Elizabeth in her misguided attempt to escape from the circumstances of her home life. Elizabeth's wish to have fun is motivated by her desire to find self-worth in a world outside her deprived family situation which has offered her little in the way of stability and self-esteem; her youth is credited for much of the confusion found in her decisions. Similar child-like impulses to break loose and find a more exciting life were found in Frankie, McCuller's youth in *The Member of the Wedding*. The wild delusions of a teen-aged girl are exposed in Frankie's erratic behavior. Her restless, unchanneled nature is in constant physical motion, compelling her at a critical moment to run away. In contrast to Elizabeth's frightened apology for her life, Frankie demands that life satisfy her; if her circumstances do not meet those demands, she will go wherever necessary to have them met with few regrets for cutting family ties.

The impulse for these characters to flee from their circumstances in the hope of finding a new life elsewhere is often motivated by fear. Perhaps the most overwhelming anxiety, typically female and portrayed in three of the plays mentioned, is the debilitating terror of living alone in a society which emphasizes woman's dependence upon men. Sara expresses her dread of a life-long existence without Kurt. In *Hope for a Harvest* Carlotta explains that her reasons for coming back home were based on her inability to live with herself alone. Her strength to deal with life has begun to break down because of her fears of being alone, of getting old alone. And Frankie experiences the depths of isolation when the wedding is over and the couple leaves her behind.

In 1940 Franken revealed another theme peculiar to women which she personified in her characterization of the young Claudia;

the difficulties of the child-adult transition in women. Ten years later Carson McCullers presented the same theme in Frankie, the confused adolescent of her play. Frankie's fixation with the wedding couple parallels the desperate clinging that characterizes Claudia's tenacious hold on her mother. Although Frankie reaches out beyond herself while Claudia holds onto a past which is behind her, an interesting comparison can be made between the two characters on the basis of how their transitions are resolved. Just as Frankie attempts to escape from her childhood, Claudia, although no longer an adolescent, a fact which she realizes but with which she cannot seem to cope, struggles to accept responsibility for herself. Both confront shattering experiences which destroy their dreams of perpetual bliss; Frankie is prevented from sharing a new life with her brother, and Claudia's dream of continual happiness dissolves when she learns of her mother's fatal illness. Both are taught lessons in reality by death and change, and both find the inner resources to meet the challenges in ways which assist their progression into adulthood. Frankie finds a new friend and a new home; Claudia begins to understand and accept the pattern of life and death and is able to release her hold on her mother and find happiness in anticipation of her own motherhood.

Both characters are frankly curious about their own sexuality and their physical attractiveness. Frankie worries that she may offend her peers and so douses herself periodically with perfume; when she is rejected by the neighborhood girls' club, she rushes out to sprinkle herself again. She worries about being too tall, attempts to stretch her sheared hair to look more feminine, and fantasizes about becoming a movie star or fashion model. She is fascinated by Berenice's stories of Ludie, the only man Berenice has ever loved, who, because he died the same month and year that Frankie was born, forms a strong mystical image of men in Frankie's mind. The tales of Berenice's many boyfriends intrigue her, but she will not believe the secrets her peers tell her about adult sexual relations.

The "child-bride" Claudia is beset with the same unformed self-image. She doubts her ability to attract men in spite of her obvious charm and naturalness and wishes her husband to think of her more as a sex symbol than as just a wife. She experiments with

the bachelor writer who lives nearby, innocently enjoying his advances and even more innocently explaining her reactions to her
bewildered husband. She welcomes the suggestions of her more
worldly friends who attempt to teach her the art of seduction
through dress and makeup. Like Frankie, she is uncertain of the
impression she makes on others and so seeks definition by artifical
means. Both Frankie and Claudia garb themselves in tasteless, ludicrous clothing which they hope will improve their images, but both
experience miserable failure.

Both characters learn they must draw on inner resources in
order to meet crises. Frankie's crises, the rejection by the wedding
couple of her offer to live with them and the death of John Henry,
precipitate positive results, however. The two events represent potential barriers to her growth but when she overcomes them by
finding the "we" of herself in new friends, they lead to the new
experiences for which she has been longing. Although she loses her
connections with perhaps the one person who loves her most, Bere-
enice, she leaves her childhood prepared to face other crises in her
adult life.

Claudia's problem has been her difficulty in facing the fig-
urative loss of her mother as well as the physical loss. Her strength
is derived from an inner resource which, up to this point, she has
never had to exercise; when she finds how to accept life's inevitabil-
ities she is able to face her dilemma and regain her faith in herself.
Like Frankie, she is able to deal with a negative experience by
finding its positive value. The experience of a woman's transition
from childhood to adulthood is rarely discussed by male writers.
Both Franken and McCullers in presenting ostensibly simple themes,
expressed this conflicting experience found in all women's lives thus
validated an authentic, universal human problem.

Of the nine plays considered during this decade, *The Member
of the Wedding* was perhaps the most distinctive in style and most
universal in theme. Its form and content were innovative in introducing the possibility that such a loosely constucted drama dealing
with a simple plot could be successful on a Broadway stage. Often
the play was described by critics as being no play at all since there

was no sense of resolution or climax to the work and because it dealt with the seemingly insignificant problems of a youth going through puberty. But the play is not so much a theatre piece as it is, as Margaret Marshall, theatre critic for *The Nation*, describes it, "whatever in the theatre corresponds to the tone poem in music;" as Marshall views it, it is an elaborate orchestration of authentic experience, seeming to have no fixed form, but based upon the descriptive theme of adolescent loneliness.[3]

Perhaps the most outstanding aspect of McCullers' drama which contributed much to the value of woman-centered interests was in the play's simultaneous universality. McCullers' intention was not to write a "woman's play," but to expose common truths of adolescent awareness through the character sketch of Frankie, who, curiously, seems at times to think, talk, act and even look like a boy. Rosalind Miles suggested that McCullers' aim, in addition to giving us the portrait of the development of a consciousness, was also to concentrate on the individual, "the parochial even," to the degree that her story opened up as a fable and assumed the status of "timeless, placeless narratives" found somewhere in the realm of human experience.[4] Thus it seems that it was the playwright's purpose in presenting a human condition of life as found in an individual to explicate the universal sense of isolation. The hazards of Frankie's existence are found within herself, and her reactions to the abstract values, the weight of time, "bolts of chance," unexplained phenomena, compel the play's action. With *The Member of the Wedding*, McCullers broadened the scope for women writers in dealing with a theme peculiar to her sex but declaring it as a theme which embraced all human understanding.

The decade between 1940 and 1950 was an economically and politically cataclysmic period in the United States. The effects of war and post-war reconstruction were the major preoccupations of dramatists who attempted to sort out the resultant confusion of the time. Women playwrights, although seeming to experience more opportunities in the first half of the decade in having their works produced, were limited in their interests in women as leading dramatic characters since much of their attention was drawn to the demand for upholding political and moral ideologies. The female characters of such war-theme plays as *Watch on the Rhine, The Searching Wind*, and *Hope for a Harvest*, and post-war consciousness-raising works as *Goodbye, My Fancy*, were generally portrayed as supportive of the American ideals of democracy and morality.

In general the women playwrights of the 1940s presented positive views of women in a variety of new and unconventional roles. Interestingly, these new roles for which women had seemed to be asking the decade before created as many conflicts in the characters' lives perhaps because the situation of woman's equality was never resolved. This was evidenced by the call for women to return to their domestic worlds and relinquish their jobs outside the home to the returning male members of society after peace had been established.

But this short-lived change did afford women the opportunity to view themselves in positions which they had seldom, if ever, held. During this decade the main female characters in the works considered ran the occupational gamut from politican to juvenile delinquent; only two dominant female characters, Claudia, from the Franken drama, and Sara, from *Watch on the Rhine*, filled the conventional role of wife-mother, but both were drawn with qualifications.

The post-war female ideal emerged during this time and was recognized by Faye Kanin as an authentic image upon which to base her ultra-feminine politician character in *Goodbye, My Fancy*. Lois W. Banner in her book, *Women in Modern America*, noted that one of the consistent themes of the 1940s in entertainment involved the hard-driving professional woman who was eventually shown that sex and marriage were more important than a successful career. These portrayals, she noted, although anti-feminist in their viewpoint, did "strike a new note":

> The women... were portrayed as strong-minded, quick-witted, even aggressive. Despite the fact that ... [they] ... regularly gave in to men ... their intelligence and strength showed through. They were women of character and force. ... In fact, so much does the personality of these women dominate ... that their ultimate surrender seems almost irrelevant.[5]

This was Agatha Reed; and from this image women were shown a new kind of prototype. Even though the image did not "open the vision of a feminist future" to the wives and mothers of the post-war era, Banner declared, their projection was not unrelated to the emergence of the feminism of the 1960s.[6]

By the end of the decade McCullers saw universal dramatic appeal in the less aggrandized circumstances of women's lives. Although Henry Hewes concluded that the theatre of this decade ended generally in a neurotic, self-conscious state, McCullers' work introduced a new phase of writing by women dramatists.

During the 1950s, only four dramas by women sustained runs on Broadway of over thirty performances. They were Hellman's *The Autumn Garden* and *Toys in the Attic*, Jane Bowles' *In the Summer House*, and Lorraine Hansberry's *A Raisin in the Sun*. Although these four plays were a small representation of women's writing during this decade, they were representative of some of the strongest and most intelligent writing of all the dramatists considered in this study.

The ten years between 1950 and 1960 were characterized by inconsistencies and fluctuations in society and economics; a parallel situation developed in the theatre in which, paradoxically, some of the worst plays were presented along with some of the best American dramas. The general feeling in the theatre was one of groping for new ways of dealing with the paradoxical times. And yet the arbitrary elimination of many new works through the "hit or flop" system which had taken hold of the theatre was a major factor in the discouragement of playwrights from developing their talents. To add to the already present difficulties in having their works produced, playwrights were confronted by the fact that the decision to produce a new play often was based on how successful a play might be in terms of financial return to its backers and producers and not necessarily on its artistic merits or its social concerns. As a result there were fewer opportunities available for playwrights to have their works produced on professional stages.

The situation seemed critical for women writers whose

numbers dropped drastically during this decade, although a few women were finding moderate success in light, domestic comedies. For serious dramatists, however, this discouraging situation seemed complicated further by the still prevalent post-war attitude which stressed the need for women to go back into the domestic scene and out of the professional world. Banner emphasized the two central and divergent trends which influenced women's lives in the two decades following the Second World War: women's continued participation in the work force, and a resurgent cultural emphasis on domesticity and femininity as woman's proper role.[7]

Bitter anti-feminist thought had occurred directly after the war in which the importance of marriage and motherhood was stressed. At this time feminist rebuttal to the arguments of traditionalists was weak since the majority of Americans had become conservative in opinion and lifestyle.[8] Yet one of the paradoxes of the decade was the fact that more and more women were entering the work force, and there was a general awareness that there was discontent among women who spent most of their time at home. To meet this frustration, a trend toward educating women to find more satisfaction in their "natural role" and recognize the housewife as a professional began but, as Banner notes, these efforts had little impact on popular attitudes. Banner refers to this period as the "back-to-home" movement in which, on a popular level, the new emphasis on domesticity was everywhere apparent and the national feminine model was the homemaker.[9] She also points out that the deprivation of the war years had made a close family life attractive and women were eager to re-establish family security for their returning soldiers. By the mid-1950s the overt anti-feminism of the immediate post-war years had ended, leaving "practically no feminist spark" among American women.[10]

Concurrent with the shift of importance from the externalities of women's lives to their inner conflicts was a literary development which emphasized the psychological study of characters; the new trend, finding its way in the theatre, formed what critics termed "the new drama," originating in the works of playwrights such as Tennessee Williams, but, according to some theorists, rooted actually in the plays of Anton Chekhov. Two of the three women dramatists studied during this time were critically analyzed on the basis of how the new trend influenced their works. Lillian Hellman and Jane Bowles offered new perspectives on psychological levels, Hellman modeling her experimentation after Chekhov as a device to perfect her craft and Bowles advocating the "new drama" as a means to express the importance of examining the tormented subconscious world of her characters.

Hellman, attempting to loosen the tight construction of her earlier works and widen her playwriting horizons, experimented with Chekhovian dialogue and situations; as a result she produced two plays, *The Autumn Garden* and *Toys in the Attic. The Autumn Garden*, while demonstrating strong dramatic qualities, was the less successful experiment of the two. Lee Strasberg defended its diffusion and unresolved characters by pointing out that its indirectness was intended to place emphasis on the characters and their inner conflicts rather than underscore the outward drama.[11] In order to be staged consistently with Hellman's intentions, said Strasberg, Hellman's play demanded a new environment to accomodate the sense of continuous action which the characters seemed to create even after their dialogue stopped.[12] So, as a playwright searching for a new means to express herself, Hellman was also sponsoring the need to re-evaluate the visual elements of the theatre in order to meet the demands of the increasing numbers of experimental styles.

In *Toys in the Attic* Hellman's perceptions of Chekhovian drama were more fully realized in theme and purpose. Hewes remarked that formerly Hellman might have turned her tale of the hapless young brother and the two indigent sisters into her usual melodramatic form by causing Julian to see his weaknesses, attempt to extricate himself from his dependency, and fail; this approach would have been more dramatic and more typically Hellman. But, Hewes observed that her concern for recording life precisely as she saw it outweighed the inclination to rouse sympathetic response.[13] In the minds of many critics objectivity was clearly difficult for Hellman, but it had been most fully realized in this work.

Jane Bowles also offered an alternative to the "well-made" formula of theatrical realism. As a novelist and short story writer she possessed several strong characteristics: subtlety, sensitivity, economy of style, and originality. These qualities were harmonious with the "new drama" trend, and, in making the shift from fiction to dramatic writing, she became known as a proponent of that school. Indeed, in her play, *In the Summer House*, style took precedence over movement and form and the neurotic twists and turns in the minds of her women created the more important aspect of the play, its atmosphere. Kronenberger believed that although *In the Summer House* had very much its own style, it had too little of its own substance, a typically negative criticism directed toward many of the followers of the "new drama."[14] For this reason her characters were often evaluated as contrivances rather than creations. But Bowles, like other writers who embraced this new dramatic form, was concerned chiefly with establishing her characters from the center of their sub-consciousness. Clurman perceived the technique as a means of getting directly to the primitive impulses of human beings which he described as essentially a poetic approach, as valid as, if less understandable than, the more than rational elements of characterization found in realistic drama.[15] Moreover, Bowles' preoccupation with her characters' psychology effectively demonstrated their emotional isolation, apparently this being the playwright's main concern.

Even though Bowles exhibited a sympathetic view toward her character, Gertrude, and Hellman endeavored to maintain objectivity with the Bernier sisters, both playwrights displayed similar thematic patterns which shaped their creative expression. Emphasizing the often helpless, sometimes deranged makeup of their characters, both contributed a deeply felt understanding of the fears of troubled personalities. Bowles, for example, depicted the psychological disintegration of a woman who fails in her efforts to impose strict control over her life as well as the lives of others. In her childhood desperation to be accepted by her father Gertrude has mimicked his arid self-containment, denying any true emotion in herself as an adult. To lose control over Molly and lose contact with her father's standards are her greatest fears. Her daily regimen and even the food she eats must adhere to her code of self-discipline. For her, lack of control leads to insanity, the loosening of the bonds, which she relates through her peculiar twisted introversion. She is suspicious of Molly because she looks like her Latin father, and all Latins, Gertrude observes, are irresponsible and wild. To Gertrude, who is red-haired, dark hair and dark features are an indication of sinister and uncontrolled qualities.

Gertrude's gradual disintegration begins with the breaking down of the superficialities of her physical world. Her relationship with the uninhibitied Mexican family forces her to change her lifestyle; instead of light salads, she is surfeited with heavy exotic meals which the Mexican women literally dump in her lap; the Solares women surround her, teasing her with their antic behavior, oblivious to her strict rules of decorum; their love of pleasure threatens her discipline ethic.

Because she loses control over her outer world, her inner world collapses too. She is no longer able to conjure her father's image because it was false to begin with. She loses her power over Molly because her strength, which was also false, breaks down, and Molly is not able to accept her as the frightened, exhausted woman she really is. Ironically, the means by which she attempts to save herself from insanity are the cause of her mental breakdown.

Bowles' characterization of Gertrude cannot escape the suggestion of Freudian psychoanalysis, but the playwright's interest in the evolution of Gertrude's neurotic state is founded in her compassionate vision of life and her sympathy with a suffering individual.

Similarly, Hellman revealed that Carrie's fears are the forces which motivate her self-centered actions. She is jealous of Lily's hold on Julian and envious of her unorthodox behavior. Annoyed by Lily's naive attempt at "girlish confidences," Carrie angrily reveals her hidden fears. She tells Lily that she is frightened of her hair "which isn't nice anymore," of her job "which isn't there any more," and "of praying for small things and knowing just how small they are."[16] The expression of her fears forces her to discover that she and Anna have locked themselves away from the world perhaps because they were frightened of saying or hearing more than they could stand. Hellman is in sympathy with Carrie's desperation; this is most evident when Carrie cries out: "There are lives that are shut and should stay shut, you hear me, and people who should not talk about themselves, and that was us."[17]

But the playwright urges no action to resolve her characters' difficulties. The uncontrovertible truth of Carrie is that she cannot change; she will not learn how to deal with her fears from this one episode in her life. As Hellman's vision of human behavior allows, Carrie will remain as she is, finding other ways to carry on the pattern of her unrealized life. She already resets the pattern of deception in the last speeches of the play after Julian has been beaten and Anna returns. "Let's be glad nothing worse has happened," Carrie says; "We're together, the three of us, that's all that matters."[18]

During this decade, Bowles and Hellman, as well as Lorraine Hansberry, all indicated their interest in women's lives by basing dramatic conflict in confrontations. In *The Autumn Garden*, Sophie, the realistic German refugee, is intolerant of Nina's largesse when Nina offers her money to return to Europe. She recognizes Nina's need to reinforce the noble ánd long-suffering false image she has of herself. Because she does not want to be a contributor to the artifices and stratagems of the Denery marriage, she forces Nina to realize that, as Nick's wife, she has accepted the role of the honorable lady who stays behind to discharge her obligations and then goes off to forgive her disobedient husband.

Lena's perceptions of her daughter, Beneatha, in Hansberry's *A Raisin in the Sun*, are keenly felt, but the two women often come to understand one another by unspoken means. When Beneatha unwittingly mocks Lena's religious faith, exclaiming that there is no God, a single action from Lena re-establishes authority, although no words pass between them: after considering what her daughter has just said, Lena rises and crosses slowly to her daughter, then powerfully and deliberately slaps her across the face. There is only silence between them but a tacit understanding has taken place as Beneatha accedes to matriarchal jurisdiction.

A similar confrontation between mother and daughter is presented in Bowles' drama. At the end of the play as she restrains Molly, Gertrude stops in mid-sentence and realizes that by confessing her weaknesses, she has destroyed Molly's dependence on her. The sudden understanding coming to both women is symbolized by their actions; Gertrude slowly releases Molly who, upon realizing the significance of this gesture, rushes off. Gertrude offers no resistance even though she knows Molly will never return.

The most abstract confrontation is between Carrie and Anna in *Toys in the Attic*. By forcing the two behind their mutual blind of empty trivialities, Hellman produces the strange effect of making them seem like one and the same person. This phenomenon is adumbrated in Albertine's observation: "Sometimes I can't tell which of you is speaking," she says; "It's as if you had exchanged faces, back and forth, forth and back."[19] Indeed, before Anna's departure the two become alter-egoes of each other as they confront the shared deceptions of their life together. Neither one has ever acted independently of the other; they have remained together with the hope of eventually finding another way to live. But this has been sheer hypocrisy and, when the small details and duties of their lives can no longer hide their frustrations, there is no longer a substantial connection between them.

The spent and wasted lives of Hellman's women of *The Autumn Garden*, and Carrie and Anna, as well as Bowles' Gertrude and Mrs. Constable, contrast with the full and hopeful life of Lena Younger, the matriarch of *A Raisin in the Sun*. Hellman's women have all based their lives either on dreams which will never be fulfilled because of their inherent inability to make them materialize or upon lies which hide true motives. After having lived with their deprivations and sacrifices for so long they have come to prefer them over the things they thought they wanted. Constance realizes that being alone is no way to live but her effort to give Crossman the opportunity to propose marriage to her is self-effacing and half-hearted. The wants of Carrie and Anna have been self-deceiving devices; when Julian provides them, they are appalled and embarrassed by his extravagance. Gertrude unwittingly destroys the source which feeds her delusion, her relationship with Molly. As she recounts her losses, she deceives herself again by remembering her life with Molly as happy and productive. With the death of Vivian, Mrs. Constable has been released from the last devitalizing relationship, but she loses herself through the effects of alcohol because she is incapable of coping with her new freedom.

But Lena Younger is capable of acting upon her dreams of establishing a new home and a new life for herself and her children. She has faced her troubles realistically and has maintained a solid base of integrity upon which her character has been founded. Her hopes have endured, as she has, through her capacity to refuse to be beaten by hardship. Hansberry's optimism is clearly sounded through Lena who, even though her principles are threatened by her son's foolish speculations, is the steadfast force welding her family together as a solid unit.

Although the three women playwrights who represented the 1950s were neither pro- nor anti-feminist in their examinations of the lives of women, their work reflected the persistence of the personal struggles in which American women were involved during this time. Continuing to write of domestic situations, they experimented nevertheless with material which probed deeper into the inner lives of their women characters and revealed many of the feminine neuroses brought about by the changing times. All three playwrights addressed the question of where the spinster, the widow, the unloved wife might fit into a post-war society. From this they disclosed various feminine conditions ranging from neurosis, alcoholic release, mental derangement, incest, and marital unrest to moral strength, stability, compassion, and courage. The notion of the past decade that women's problems could be solved through marriage and the establishment of a home had been supplanted by this time with the apparent concern of these playwrights to examine the processes which led individuals to their actions, traits, and attitudes. Although most of the characters studied from these select plays were aimless women with weak domestic roots and few family ties, the solutions to their problems were sought through their individual consciousnesses rather than from the conventionality of their social roles. Perhaps the most important development in women playwrights during this decade was their response to the uneasy position of women in American society; by experimenting with new themes and forms, as well as revitalizing traditional ones, the base for feminine dramatic study was broadened. Seeing women in alternate life styles and exploring the inherent problems which grew from those situations seemed important to playwrights such as Bowles and Hellman. Although Hansberry was disciplined by traditional rules of plot, character, and theme, her female protagonist, Lena, was a universal representative of moral strength and dignity; in fact, critic Richard Hayes was prompted to point out that with *A Raisin in the Sun* Hansberry indicated not only a non-sexed view of human struggle with its ultimte resolution but a non-racial one as well.[20]

The political, economic, and social ills of the 1950s extended into the following decade, prompting theatre critic and historian Robert Brustein to define the 1960s as the "seasons of discontent." This proved to be an appropriate designation for the works of women playwrights during this era. Against a background of social unrest which resulted in public remonstration for numerous issues (e. g., environmental pollution, poverty, civil rights, youth protests, the Vietnam War, and overpopulation), a large representation of women writers sought the means by which to express their reactions to these circumstances as well as a way in which to express their personal grievances. Minority groups, dissidents, left-wing activists, and others had provided the decade with a reform mentality which was adopted by several women writers who identified strongly with many of the causes being expressed. Conventional attitudes and traditions were being questioned and, for women, the period of the sixties was a particularly explosive time.

The strong appeal of domesticity in the 1950s was suddenly countered by virulent extremes of militant feminism in the 1960s. The radical reaction was not surprising considering several resurgent forces which contributed to this most current feminist activity. Banner suggested that many women were ready to accept a radical ideology which supported changes in women's social standing because this was a period of outspoken causes and many Americans were receptive to controversial exposé; for women the impetus was heightened by cultural and political attacks from both conservative and reform fronts.

In the theatre of the 1960s a wave of experimentation with new themes, forms, styles, and methods had developed. With the emergence of the new feminism, a more emphatic voice was heard from women in the arts and many women playwrights were quick to adopt reform methods since they too were involved in challenging customary practices of social life. Believing that their uneasy society demanded a new response from its artists, these experimentalists personified the causes and effects of the changing position of women. Apparently they felt that the popular form of domestic comedy was failing to understand and take seriously the deeper conflicts of this problematic and rebellious age and of the special situation of women who were caught in it. Off-Broadway stages proved to be an accessible and sympathetic outlet for their work and an increased number of women were drawn to the smaller theatres to present their new modes of expression.

Of the plays studied from the 1960-1970 decade, much can be said of their importance statistically. Three of the five off-Broadway works were recipients of distinguished play awards ("Obie" awards); they were *Home Movies, Viet Rock*, and *Futz*. Kennedy's *Funnyhouse of a Negro* not only promoted further regard for the black woman playwright, but was also the first experimental play of this era written by a woman to attract a substantial audience and continue a run of over thirty performances. Myrna Lamb's *The Mod Donna* represented the feminist views of an increasingly significant portion of the American populace while forcefully reflecting a changing image of women in American society.

According to Harriet Kriegel, women playwrights, then, in questioning their position as spokeswomen for the new social movements, sought to create new heroines for women. As seen by an examination of the serious dramatic literature of the 1950s, the theatre, having been previously occupied with world conflict, began to focus its attention on the private worlds and inner struggles of its characters. But for women characters this preoccupation, according to Kriegel, developed into the "feminine mystique" of the late fifties and early sixties.[21] New heroines had been created by a culture which divided its image of woman between "the grotesque sexuality of a Marilyn Monroe" and the "antiseptic virginity of a Debbie Reynolds."[22] Thus it seems that the new images proved no more satisfying than previous ones. Female characters were still defined by how they adapted to a masculine-oriented society, their own creativity and autonomy still being secondary considerations.

Finding themselves still "dehumanized" and "mythicized out of proportion" on the stage, several women playwrights offered what they considered to be new concepts of American womanhood.[23] Believing that in the past playwrights had depicted women as either predators or goddesses, these images being derived from a well-established tradition, they attempted to view women through a heightened consciousness. Adrienne Kennedy portrayed her feminine protagonist, Sarah, as a representative of the divided ethnic mind. The fact of her femininity is adjunct to the major problem of mixed allegiances and confused identity, this problem eventuating in Sarah's desire to be completely unidentifiable. Kennedy's concern was with the guilt complexes of a fragmented self, and her writing was pervaded by an intense search for a means to unite that self.

Lorraine Hansberry also suggested a deeper insight into feminine thinking in *The Sign in Sidney Brustein's Window*. Although Iris effectively exhibits destructive tendencies in her relationship with Sidney, she is neither predator nor goddess. She destroys Sidney's renewed hopes but by the same means with which he has shaken hers: she tells the truth. Furthermore, she rebels against the false image which Sidney has created of her, the mountain girl who represents freedom to him, an unrealistically frustrating image considering the fact that her dreams of recognition are deferred also, just as his fantasies have been. She is self-obsessed and defensive to be sure, but Hansberry equated these qualities with Sidney's weaknesses and both have been drawn compassionately as fragile human beings passionately involved in the balance of human relations.

Yet the drama which was spawned from this era of new feminist thought reflected other trends which were prevalent during the 1960s, for example, the questioning of political systems and the disenchangment with social institutions. Megan Terry's *Viet Rock* was one of the few theatrical presentations of the 1960s to attempt to arouse social conscience by protesting the war in Vietnam. Portraying the dehumanization of participants in the war and relying on a mocking parody of its indignities, Terry proposed a variation on the themes of propagandistic theatre with an emphasis on the coinciding efforts of playwright and actor to draw free association one from the other as the substance of the work.

Rosalyn Drexler and Rochelle Owens offered depersonalized characters for the sake of showing the broader concerns of the breakdown of social institutions and the underlying cruelty of man's behavior toward his fellow man. The nonsense characters of Drexler's *Home Movies* were created with the serious intention of breaking with convention. As a result they are purely superficial figures of fantasy and wit, creating "anything can happen" surroundings. Imposed identities and decorous roles in this way are resisted and their validity denied. In addition, one-line rejoinders demonstrate Drexler's use of language as "red herring."[24]

Rochelle Owens, depicting the cruelty of a conformist world in *Futz*, called for a return to man's basic instincts where could be found, she believed, the salvation of the human and the humane.[25] The gross creatures who inhabit Owens' bizarre world personify the irrational impulses of man which, in her view, are a truer depiction of humanity than the mirroring of man's false aspirations and socially constricted code of behavior.

But perhaps the most impressive expression was the changing attitudes of women towards themselves and their society, the most forceful evidence of this being Myrna Lamb's *The Mod Donna*. Lamb's work depicted the "unholy merry-go-round" of two women, both mesmerized by their own sense of themselves as merely sexual creatures.[26] All the obsessions of female experience are presented in order that Lamb may refute them in her chorus finale. The demand for "liberation" supercedes all other philosophies, categories, or expectations of women.

Lamb's views were representative of the underlying anger which propelled the feminist movement into such radical outcry in the 1960s. In *The Mod Donna* the two-dimensional soap opera characters are confined by the definitions of their modern marriages to the disadvantage of both sexes, but with the women portrayed as the eternal and ultimate losers. Lashing out at male supremacy,

Lamb denounced all social institutions, including marriage, which encouraged women to seek identification soley through sex. Marriage, above all, was the "beautiful cop-out for a woman."[27]

Most of the activities of women playwrights in this decade took place in the off-Broadway houses. Adrienne Kennedy's *Funnyhouse of a Negro*, Rosalyn Drexler's *Home Movies*, Megan Terry's *Viet Rock*, Rochelle Owens' *Futz*, and Myrna Lamb's *The Mod Donna* were all products of off-Broadway playhouses and helped to further the goals of the radical "underground" theatre, the new movement which rebelled against the well-made, social realism and psychological probing of the Ibsen-O'Neill tradition.

Lorraine Hansberry's *The Sign in Sidney Brustein's Window* was the only long-running play to be produced on a Broadway stage and to meet the expectations of the conventional three-act form which held sway over the legitimate stage. But even her exploration of the mind of her main female character indicated a profound concern for the difficulties of a woman caught between the desire to keep a marriage intact and the need for self-fulfillment and maturity.

It is unfortunate that Megan Terry's 1970 work, *Approaching Simone,* cannot be included in this list of women's plays running over thirty performances on or off-Broadway stages. The play, produced in Boston and New York, ran a total of only nine performances; however, it received recognition as one of Terry's best plays, receiving the "Obie" award in 1970. It is of pivotal importance in this study of American women playwrights since it presents a radically different female protagonist. Terry's biographical characterization is based on the experiences of Simone Weil, the French Jewess who died during the second world war in France after writing several books, essays, letters, and poetry in support of her humanistic and anti-Nazi views.

Terry seemed concerned with the fact that in the patriarchal society of America, American women were forced to imitate masculine models in literature since there were few great women figures whose human identity had been expressed in terms of their intellect.

Most female protagonists, the playwright contended, were presented in terms of sexual conflict whereby their identities were described by their conflicting relationships with men. By choosing Simone Weil as the central figure for this work, Terry hoped to offer to women a spiritually strong individual who forces herself to struggle for creative expression while overcoming the acute, socially imposed limitations of being a woman. Kriegel described Simone as a highly intelligent woman who attempts, by her own sacrifice, to bring specific meaning to Christ's sacrifice.[28] Indeed, Terry's character, the first "totally self-aware" protagonist to appear in any of her plays, as well as her "first heroic figure," exemplifies Terry's concept of total liberation for a woman brought about by the efforts of her own will.[29]

The activity among women playwrights which occurred during th 1960s was an encouraging indication of the increasing importance of the contribution of women writers to current theatre trends. Most of the playwrights examined from this era were representatives of the "underground" theatre and were attempting a strong defense of their views of social ills and psychic exploration. Not only were these women responding to a new social environment but were becoming aware of new perceptions of themselves as well. They were also attempting to assume responsibility for speaking out for themselves, testing restrictions, and extending the imposed limitations about what women could write and how, an unprecedented situation in their playwriting history. Written and produced from a wide range of styles, techniques, and forms, their plays created a strikingly different aspect of women's drama when compared to those works offered by women dramatists of the 1930s.

Although some of the playwrights of this period did not present exclusive woman-centered material (e. g., Terry's *Viet Rock* and Owens' *Futz*), others attempted to penetrate the apparently alienated world of women and discovered a valid and stage-worthy source from which to draw. All of them drew their sources from indigenous material, looked to their culture for response and responded to it, thus making the attempt at a true identification between themselves as women writers, regardless of their chosen material, and the world in which they lived.

Conclusions

Between 1930 and 1970 a pattern emerged from the playwriting efforts of selected American women playwrights which indicated that women have been a vital, contributive force in the American theatre and that throughout the past forty years they were gradually obtaining freer expression of a variety of themes and characters in spite of critical abuse and disregard. The pattern seemed to coincide with the changing roles of women in society from one decade to another.

During the 1930s women who were successful in their playwriting efforts were praised when they attempted traditional, less profound works in which their women characters were expected to uphold and maintain the socially acceptable feminine image in American society.

In the 1940s the outbreak of World War II created more opportunities for women to have their works produced as well as offering them a more expanded base of experience for their women characters. These playwrights were encouraged to uphold the standards of democracy and to assist the war effort in their writings. But the increase in the number of successful women playwrights which had occurred at that time was cut short by the war's end and by the male work force returning from the war fronts to resume occupations traditionally held by men. The few serious women writers who survived this displacement began to write deeper psychological studies of their women characters and their anxieties; this emphasis reflected some of the internal frustrations in the lives of American women whose roles often seemed ambivalent at this time.

During the decade of the 1950s most successful writing by women for the theatre came from those playwrights who wrote traditional domestic comedies; the preponderance of women comedy writers was a contrast to the few women writing serious drama who continued to investigate the minds and emotions of their women characters.

The 1960s represented a time when women began to declare

their independence from roles which seemed to suppress their individuality. Women playwrights, finding a new outlet for these expressions, contributed much to the "underground" theatre movement which embraced virtually any form or style expressing an anti-traditional approach to drama.

Similarities were found in theme from one decade to another. During the 1930s the predominant themes were social and domestic in which women were portrayed in conventional family situations and historical-romance settings, with the exception found in Lillian Hellman's *The Children's Hour*, a study of aberrant psychology and the internal struggle of two female protagonists.

Many playwrights of the 1940s were influenced by the commercial, industrial, and economic conditions brought about by World War II. During the war the subjects of national loyalty and economic disruption were presented by the majority of women. But from 1945 to 1950 attention was brought back to domestic situations; themes of family life, homebuilding, and post-war social problems concerned women dramatists at the time. Yet, rather than focusing attention on the private, domestic conflicts which the women characters of the 1930s had experienced, the characters of the 1940s represented the more general concerns of a society during post-war reconstruction. Delinquency among teenagers, environmental concerns, war prevention, and the new post-war image of woman were dealt with in these plays.

Similarly, the years between 1950 and 1960 were characterized by many social and political inconsistencies and fluctuations. In order to deal with these changes, new forms were explored in the theatre. It was a critical point in the development of women playwrights, for the "hit or flop" system which had enveloped the Broadway stage was a discouraging situation for new and unknown playwrights. Also, anti-feminist thought prevailed which sponsored the concepts that marriage and motherhood were of primary importance to women rather than professional careers. The number of successful women playwrights dropped drastically during this time. Nevertheless, the few women remaining displayed a shift of thematic importance from the externalities of their characters' lives to their inner conflicts. Often women were seen as helpless, sometimes deranged, psychologically disturbed individuals, and most of the characters were non-conforming, unattached women living alone.

Unlike the playwrights of the 1930s, 1940s, and the early 1950s, the playwrights of the 1960s, the majority of them rebelling against well-made, social realism and psychological probing, attempted a defense of their views of social ills and psychic exploration. Like the playwrights of the past decades they responded to their changing social environment but were also aware of new perceptions of themselves as well. Assuming responsiblity for the strong views which they held and which they expressed in their works, they tested traditional restrictions and extended imposed limitations. Reflecting the social unrest of the time, they took positions on such issues as poverty, civil rights, and war in Vietnam, women's rights, and other issues. Conventional attitudes and traditions, particularly those of woman's role in society, were questioned. The organization of a women's liberation front helped bring to light some inequities in women's social standing and lent further impetus to the efforts of those playwrights who supported feminist goals.

An interest in women's lives was demonstrated in many of the works investigated. In the 1930s, the dominant characters in the dramas by women were women, but the effects of dominance-oppression in male-female social problems remained much the same as before the passage of the Right to Vote Amendment in the 1920s. Women did not seem to be writing in protest for certain rights for their sex; however, many of them depicted their characters in unresolved situations which plagued American women at that time, such problems as illegitimacy, marital incompatability, maternity, and the social alienation and ostracization of nonconforming women. The actions of the plays studied from this time focused on the relationship of woman to her family, society, or history, or on the relationship of one woman to another.

By contrast, the works of the early 1940s offered few opportunities for women to be central figures mainly because of the preoccupation of the playwrights with the war and its consequences. Women at this time were portrayed as the mainstays of national morals who upheld their positions as "Angel at the Hearth" with strength, dignity, and courage. After the war women again focused on women as central characters. But like the characters of the 1930s, these individuals suffered from the bewilderment of female identity.

The writers of the 1950s appeared to be searching for ways to redefine feminine roles in order to match the redefinition which women had actually experienced as a result of social changes. Unlike the writers of the 1930s who seemed more concerned with finding ways to resolve their characters' dilemmas through conventional feminine attitudinizing, these playwrights attempted to evaluate the psychological effects of change in women's lives. As a result, most of the dramas studied were centered in conflicts in the feminine consciousness. A particular similarity emerged in comparing the works of the 1930s with those of the 1950s when, at both times, women could devote their thoughts exclusively to the problems of their sex. The women playwrights of both eras presented views of women in the conventional roles of wives and mothers, but also emphasized the particular problems of spinsters, divorcées, career women, and widows. This awareness that conventional roles often did not seem to offer them the opportunity to explore human conflict was evidenced by the choices these playwrights made in placing their characters in non-conventional social roles. In order to present compelling dramatic material it seemed necessary to present them as antisocial figures in quest for freedom of choice. While the playwrights of the 1930s resolved these dilemmas by compromise, those of the 1950s presented less romanticized resolutions. The earlier dramas often resolved conflicts by finding superficial solutions to their protagonists' struggles, thereby absorbing their characters into the prevailing social mainstream; but in those plays of the 1950s the resolution was usually found in psychological confusion and sometimes eventual breakdown, self-delusion, or failure. The expedient happy ending was not necessarily an acceptable device for the alleviation of characters' difficulties as it had been for many of the dramas of the earlier decade.

Again, in the 1960s, emphasis shifted from woman-centered expression to that which encompassed many social problems. Like the period of the early forties when topical war-time concerns prevailed, the 1960s witnessed the expression of various points of view and opinions about specific social and political problems. Women wrote of society's ills and much of the writing seemed to personify the causes and effects of the changing position of women in America. In their view the superficial versions of women which had been depicted in the popular comedies of the Broadway stage, often reinforced by women comedy writers, had failed to understand and take seriously the deeper conflicts of the age and the special situation of women who were involved in these conflicts. The new playwrights of this era established themselves as spokeswomen for the social causes which they espoused and sought new views which would reveal women as creative, feeling individuals whose struggles and aspirations they considered to be valid dramatic material. New concepts of American womanhood seemed to emerge, and characters were drawn not from their outward social standing but from areas of thought which included the confusion of identity and the unrealistic imposition of certain identities based upon sexuality which had not been openly challenged before. Uncomfortable with a standard portrayal of women as merely sexual creatures, many of the playwrights attempted to tear down and to rebel against the kind of definition which emphasized women as sexual objects. Some dramatists indicated that male supremacy was the cause of woman's predicament.

In reviewing the effects of social changes on the characterizations of women playwrights, it was found that some dramatists sought to create new heroines for women since the images of the past seemed no longer applicable or accurate. Some of the playwrights of the 1960s felt that female characters were still being defined by how they adapted to a masculine-oriented society; they attempted to view women through the heightened consciousness at which the new wave of feminism was aiming. This study ends with a statement of the underlying anger held by some women playwrights towards the traditional views of women in conventional supportive roles; their denunciation of any social institutions which encouraged women to seek identification solely through sex, including marriage, was expressed strongly.

In brief, the American woman playwright depicted women

characters in many roles. They portrayed them as society's dependents, dramatizing their conflicts and resolving their struggles by finding means to make their anti-social behavior seem conformable to the limits of their societies. Clare Boothe, Rachel Crothers, Rose Franken, and Fay Kanin all presented women who were sophisticated, worldly, and attractive. But their leading characters could not find satisfaction in leading lives of non-conformity. All four playwrights sought means to fit their characters into conforming patterns. Their plays, *The Women, Susan and God, Outrageous Fortune*, and *Goodbye, My Fancy* all pointed to expedient resolutions.

Women were depicted as the keepers of society's standards and as the protectors of its moral strength during times of personal and national crises. The women of Lillian Hellman's *Watch on the Rhine*; Sophie Treadwell's "earth-mother" Carlotta of *Hope for a Harvest*; the indomitable matriarch, Lena, from Lorraine Hansberry's *A Raisin in the Sun*, all were personifications of dignity and strength amidst troubled environments.

Emphasis shifted to the changing roles of women who began to question their position as social dependents. Franken's Claudia, Frankie from *A Member of the Wedding*, and Mrs. Constable and Molly from *In the Summer House* represented characters who questioned and were confused by their dependent statuses.

Women playwrights explored psychological effects derived from a society which had shifted women from one role to another and had caused confusion as to their true identities. This confusion, as well as its extremes, namely self-delusion and paranoia, were dramatized in Rose Franken's *Another Language*, Lillian Hellman's *The Searching Wind*, Lorraine Hansberry's *The Sign in Sidney Brustein's Window*; Megan Terry utilized depersonalized identities by creating "transformations" in her play *Viet Rock*. But the most stunning expression of confused identity was found in Adrienne Kennedy's *Funnyhouse of a Negro*.

Finally, women were seen as victims of a male-dominated society in which their lives led inevitably to dissatisfaction and frustration when they could not be accepted, or could not accept themselves, as autonomous individuals who were capable of making decisions for themselves and were able to accept responsiblity for their own lives. The wives in Myrna Lamb's *The Mod Donna*; Sydney Brustein's wife, Iris, in Hansberry's work; and Megan Terry's Simone in *Approaching Simone* all experienced the frustration of not being understood by their male counterparts while not wholly understanding themselves.

In cross-referencing the results of each decade some comparisons can be drawn. It was found, for example, that Lillian Hellman in *The Children's Hour* indicated a theme explored two decades later by Jane Bowles in *In the Summer House*: the unresolved problem of women who had conformed to social expectations (except that they were unable or unwilling to maintain a legitimate relationship, that is, marriage, with a man), but for whom society had no definite place. As women alone they were vulnerable, unhappy failures. Hellman, although attempting to change her style in the 1950s, repeated the similarity in her pessimistic view of the futures of such women in *Toys in the Attic*. Previously, such works as *The Old Maid* and *Alison's House*, both written during the same decade as *The Children's Hour*, offered the traditional resolution that a non-conforming woman showed her nobility, thus saving herself from complete failure as a human being, by enduring her fate and passively accepting whatever role society could find for her, e. g., old maid, spinster-poetess, widow, or liberated (therefore, unhappy) woman of the new century. In the 1940s Hellman, too, reiterated the traditional resolution in *Watch on the Rhine* by depicting the stoic endurance of one female character when she loses her husband to a greater cause. But Hellman, along with the playwrights of the 1950s and 1960s, stressed the importance of emotional, psychological and psychic reaction rather than repeating traditional behavior patterns in her later plays. The deeper examination of the inner lives of women began in the 1950s after the pressures of war and post-war themes had abated and with the onset of the "New Drama" which stressed the psychological processes of characterization. Although many of the plays produced during the last decade presented no more satisfying resolutions to women's problems than those of the previous decades, these works explored more fully the complexities of personality. By the 1960s when overt attacks were being made upon various social ills, the situation of women and their importance as universal characters was more clearly focused by both experimental and traditional dramas, such as Kennedy's *Funnyhouse of a Negro*, Hansberry's two plays, *A Raisin in the Sun* and *The Sign in Sidney Brustein's Window*; Lamb's *The Mod Donna*; and Terry's *Approaching Simone*.

From this summation it appears that women characters of the plays studied changed from simple, passive women who were subjugated by the demands of their societies, to complicated, active women who attempted, not always successfully, to think and act on their own.

At the present time studies have been published regarding the contributions of women to the fields of creative writing. These studies have helped to enhance the image of the woman writer and to bring attention to works which have previously been neglected, overlooked, or disregarded; however, the topic of women in the area of playwriting still awaits a similarly extensive consideration by other authors.

Notes

[1]"Weep No More, Ladies," in *The Literary Digest*, 113, No. 9 (28 May 1932), p. 17.

[2]Euphemia Van Rensselaer Wyatt, "The Drama," in *The Catholic World*, 140 (Janaury 1935), p. 466.

[3]Margaret Marshall, "Drama," in *The Nation*, 170, No. 2 (14 January 1950), p. 44.

[4]Rosalind Miles, *The Fiction of Sex* (London: Vision Press, 1974), p. 142.

[5]Lois W. Banner, *Women in Modern America, A Brief History* (San Francisco: Harcourt, Brace, Jovanovich, Inc., 1974), p. 201.

[6]*Ibid.*, p. 202.

[7]*Ibid.*, p. 211.

[8]*Ibid.*, p. 221.

[9]*Ibid.*, p. 215.

[10]*Ibid.*, p. 223.

[11]Lee Strasberg,   ed., *Famous American Plays of the 1950's* (New York: Dell Publishing Co. Inc., 1962), p. 18.

[12]*Ibid.*, p. 19.

[13]Henry Hewes, "Broadway Postscripts," in *The Saturday Review*, 43, No. 11 (12 March 1960), p. 71.

[14]Louis Kronenberger, ed., *The Best Plays of 1953-54* (New York: Dodd, Mead and Company, 1954), p. 9.

[15]Harold Clurman, "Theatre," in *The Nation*, 178, No. 3 (16 January 1954), p. 58.

[16]Lillian Hellman, "Toys in the Attic," in *Six American Plays for Today* ed. by Bennett Cerf (New York: The Modern Library, 1961), III, p. 575.

[17]*Idem.*

[18]*Ibid.*, p. 590.

[19]*Ibid.*, I, p. 520.

[20]Richard Hayes, "The Stage," in *Commonweal*, 70, No. 3 (17 April 1959), p. 82.

[21]Harriet Kriegel, ed., *Women in Drama* (New York: The New American Library, Inc., 1975), p. xxxiii.

[22]*Idem.*

[23]*Ibid.*, p. xxxvi.

[24]Rosalyn Drexler, *The Line of Least Existence and Other Plays*, with an introduction by Richard Gilman (New York: Random House, 1967), p. ix.

[25]Rochelle Owens, *Futz and What Came After* (New York: Random House, 1968), p. 245.

[26]Vivian Gornick, "Who is the Fairest of Them All?" in *The Village Voice*, 15, No. 22 (28 May 1970), p. 47.

[27]Myrna Lamb, *The Mod Donna and Scyklon Z* (New York: Pathfinder Press, Inc., 1971), p. 139.

[28]Kriegel, *Women in Drama*, p. xxxvi.

[29]Megan Terry, *Approaching Simone*, with an introduction by Phyllis Jane Wagner (New York: The Feminist Press, 1973), p. 10.

The American Woman Playwright:
A View of Criticism and Characterization

Composed in IBM Electronic Selectric Composer *Journal Roman* and printed offset by Cushing-Malloy, Incorporated, Ann Arbor, Michigan. The paper on which the book is printed is the Northwest Paper Company's *Caslon.* The book was sewn and bound in Holliston Mills' Roxite Linen by John H. Dekker and Sons, Incorporated, Grand Rapids, Michigan.

The American Woman Playwright is a Trenowyth book, the scholarly publishing division of the Whitston Publishing Company.

This edition consists in 750 casebound copies.